Stories of Success:

Paul the Peddler
(Illustrated)

Stories of Success:

Paul the Peddler
(Illustrated)

Horatio Alger, Jr.

Sumner Books
Hermosa Beach, CA

TABLE OF CONTENTS

A NOTE FROM THE PUBLISHER

Once crowned "America's most influential writer," Horatio Alger is hardly known today. Those who are familiar with him think "rags to riches," and that's about it. Most young people have never heard of him.

What an opportunity!

More than a hundred years before our contemporary self-help movement, Horatio Alger paved the way with his vivid illustrations of the keys to success and happiness. Today, Sumner Books is excited to introduce a new generation of Americans to some of the most inspirational stories ever written. Regardless of your age, you simply cannot read a Horatio Alger book without coming away with a good feeling.

Alger's books initially sold in the millions and then the tens of millions and finally the hundreds of millions. In fact, the Chicago Daily News once called Horatio Alger "America's best-selling author of all time." Sumner Books is committed to bringing to life this best-selling collection in the form of audiobooks read by professional actors and recorded with audio engineers in our studio. Our revised e-books, each with a detailed table of contents and colored illustrations, are professionally edited, including the occasional updating of phrases to make the books as easy to read today as they were when they were first published between 1865 and 1900.

Long after his death in 1899, the magazine Publishers Weekly wrote: "To call Horatio Alger Jr. America's most influential writer may seem like an overstatement ... but ... only Benjamin Franklin meant as much to the formation of the American popular mind."

Our goal is to bring back some of the influence that Alger exerted on millions of young people in America. Yes, it's retro; it's counterintuitive and totally contrary to the cynicism that has become a part of American culture. But we are proud to be leading a movement that is as positive and uplifting as the last pages of a Horatio Alger story.

Rick Newcombe
President
Sumner Books

Stories of Success

"Every man is an impossibility until he is born."
Ralph Waldo Emerson

CHAPTER I

PAUL THE PEDDLER

"Here's your prize packages! Only five cents! Money prize in every package! Walk up, gentlemen, and try your luck!"

The speaker, a boy of fourteen, stood in front of the shabby brick building, on Nassau street, which has served for many years as the New York post office. In front of him, as he stood with his back to the building, was a small basket, filled with ordinary letter envelopes, each labeled "Prize Package."

His attractive announcement, which, at that time, had also the merit of novelty—for Paul had himself hit upon the idea, and manufactured the packages, as we shall hereafter explain—drew around him a miscellaneous crowd, composed chiefly of boys.

"What's in the packages, Johnny?" asked a bootblack, with his box strapped to his back.

"Candy," answered Paul. "Buy one. Only five cents."

"There ain't much candy," answered the bootblack, with a disparaging glance.

"What if there isn't? There's a prize."

"How big a prize?"

"There's a ten-cent stamp in some of 'em. All have got something in 'em."

Influenced by this representation, the bootblack drew out a five-cent piece, and said:

"Pitch one over then. I guess I can stand it." An envelope was at once handed to him.

A ten-cent stamp, the grand prize in Paul's Prize Packages.

"Open it, Johnny," said a newsboy at his side. Twenty curious eyes were fixed upon him as he opened the package. He drew out rather a scanty supply of candy, and then turning to Paul, with a look of indignation, said:

"Where's the prize? I don't see no prize. Give me back my five cents."

"Give it to me. I'll show you," said the young merchant.

He thrust in his finger, and drew out a square bit of paper, on which was written—One Cent.

"There's your prize," he added, drawing a penny from his pocket.

"It ain't much of a prize," said the buyer. "Where's your ten cents?"

"I didn't say I put ten cents into every package," answered Paul.

"I'd burst up pretty quick if I did that. Who'll have another package? Only five cents!"

Curiosity and taste for speculation are as prevalent among children as with men, so this appeal produced its effect.

"Give me a package," said Teddy O'Brien, a newsboy, stretching out a dirty hand, containing the stipulated sum. He also was watched curiously as he opened the package. He drew out a paper bearing the words—Two Cents.

"Bully for you, Teddy! You've had better luck than I," said the bootblack.

The check was duly honored, and Teddy seemed satisfied, though the amount of candy he received probably could not have cost over half-a-cent. Still, he had drawn twice as large a prize as the first buyer, and that was satisfactory.

"Who'll take the next?" asked Paul, in a businesslike manner. "Maybe there's ten cents in this package. That's where you double your money. Walk up, gentlemen. Only five cents!"

Three more responded to this invitation, one drawing a prize of two cents, the other two of one cent each. Just then, as it seemed doubtful whether any more would be purchased by those present, a young man, employed in a Wall Street house, came out of the post office.

"What have you got here?" he asked, pausing.

"Prize packages of candy! Money prize in every package! Only five cents!"

"Give me one, then. I never drew a prize in my life."

The exchange was speedily made.

"I don't see any prize," he said, opening it.

"It's on a bit of paper, mister," said Teddy, nearly as much interested as if it had been his own purchase.

"Oh, yes, I see. Well, I'm in luck. Ten cents!"

"Ten cents!" exclaimed several of the less fortunate buyers, with a shade of envy.

"Here's your prize, mister," said Paul, drawing out a ten-cent stamp from his vest pocket.

"Well, Johnny, you do things on the square, that's a fact. Just keep the ten cents, and give me two more packages."

This Paul did with alacrity; but the Wall Street clerk's luck was at an end. He got two prizes of a penny each.

"Well," he said, "I'm not much out of pocket. I've bought three packages, and it's only cost me three cents."

The ten-cent prize produced a favorable effect on the business of the young peddler. Five more packages were bought, and the contents eagerly inspected; but no other large prize appeared. Two cents was the maximum prize drawn. Their curiosity being satisfied, the crowd dispersed; but it was not long before another gathered. In fact, Paul had shown excellent judgment in selecting the front of the post office as his place of business. Hundreds passed in and out every hour, besides those who passed by on a different destination.

Thus many ears caught the young peddler's cry—"Prize packages! Only five cents apiece!"—and made a purchase; most from curiosity, but some few attracted by the businesslike bearing of the young merchant, and willing to encourage him in his efforts to make a living. These last, as well as some of the former class, declined to accept the prizes, so that these were so much gain to Paul.

At length but one package remained, and this Paul was some time getting rid of. At last a gentleman came up, holding a little boy of seven by the hand.

"Oh, buy me the package, papa?" he said, drawing his father's attention.

"What is there in it, boy?" asked the gentleman.

"Candy," was the answer.

Alfred, for this was the little boy's name, renewed his entreaties, having, like most boys, a taste for candy.

"There it is, Alfred," said his father, handing the package to his little son.

"There's a prize inside," said Paul, seeing that they were about to pass.

"We must look for the prize by all means," said the gentleman. "What is this? One cent?"

"Yes sir"; and Paul held out a cent to his customer.

"Never mind about that! You may keep the prize."

"I want it, pa," interposed Alfred, with his mouth full of candy.

"I'll give you another," said his father, still declining to accept the proffered prize.

Paul now found himself in the enviable position of one who, at eleven o'clock, had succeeded in disposing of his entire stock in trade, and that at an excellent profit, as we soon shall see. Business had been more brisk with him than with many merchants on a larger scale, who sometimes keep open their shops all day without taking in enough to pay expenses. But, then, it is to be considered that in Paul's case expenses were not a formidable item. He had no rent to pay, for one thing, nor clerk hire, being competent to attend to his entire business single-handed. All his expense, in fact, was the first cost of his stock in trade, and he had so fixed his prices as to insure a good profit on that. So, on the whole, Paul felt very well satisfied at the result of his experiment, for this was his first day in the prize-package business.

—

6

"I guess I'll go home," he said to himself. "Mother'll want to know how I made out." He turned up Nassau street, and had reached the corner of Maiden lane, when Teddy O'Brien met him.

"Did you sell out, Johnny?" he asked.

"Yes," answered Paul.

"How many packages did you have?"

"Fifty."

"That's bully. How much you made?"

"I can't tell yet. I haven't counted up," said Paul.

"It's better'n sellin' papers, I'll bet. I've only made thirty cents the day. Don't you want to take a partner, Johnny?"

"No, I don't think I do," said Paul, who had good reason to doubt whether such a step would be to his advantage.

"Then I'll go in for myself," said Teddy, somewhat displeased at the refusal.

"Go ahead! There's nobody to stop you," said Paul.

"I'd rather go in with you," said Teddy, feeling that there would be some trouble in making the prize packages, but influenced still more by the knowledge that he had not capital enough to start in the business alone.

"No," said Paul, positively; "I don't want any partner. I can do well enough alone."

He was not surprised at Teddy's application. Street boys are as enterprising, and have as sharp eyes for business as their elders, and no one among them can monopolize a profitable business long. This is especially the case with the young street merchant. When one has had the good luck to find some attractive article which promises to sell briskly, he takes every care to hide the source of his supply from his rivals in trade. But this is almost impossible. Cases are frequent where such boys are subjected to the closest espionage, their steps being dogged for hours by boys who think they have found a good thing and are determined to share it. In the present case Paul had hit upon an idea which seemed to promise well, and he was determined to keep it to himself as long as possible. As soon as he was subjected to competition and rivalry his gains would probably diminish.

—

7

CHAPTER II

PAUL AT HOME

**New York Tenement housing much like where
Paul and his family live.**

Paul went up Centre street and turned into Pearl. Stopping before a tenement-house, he entered, and, going up two flights of stairs, opened a door and entered.

"You are home early, Paul," said a woman of middle age, looking up at his entrance.

"Yes, mother; I've sold out."

"You've not sold out the whole fifty packages?" she asked, in surprise.

"Yes, I have. I had capital luck."

"Why, you must have made as much as a dollar, and it's not twelve yet."

"I've made more than that, mother. Just wait a minute, till I've reckoned up a little. Where's Jimmy?"

"Miss Beckwith offered to take him out to walk with her, so I let him go. He'll be back at twelve."

While Paul is making a calculation, a few words of explanation and description may be given, so that the reader may understand better how he is situated.

The rooms occupied by Paul and his mother was three in number. The largest one was about fourteen feet square, and was lighted by two windows. It was covered with a neat, though well-worn, carpet; a few cane-bottomed chairs were ranged at the windows, and on each side of the table. There was a French clock on the mantel, a rocking chair for his mother, and a few inexpensive engravings hung upon the walls. There was a hanging bookcase containing two shelves, filled with books, partly school books, supplemented by a few miscellaneous books, such as "Robinson Crusoe," "Pilgrim's Progress," a volume of "Poetical Selections," an odd volume of Scott, and several others. Out of the main room opened two narrow chambers, both together of about the same area as the main room. One of these was occupied by Paul and Jimmy; the other by his mother.

Those who are familiar with the construction of a New York tenement-house will readily understand the appearance of the rooms into which we have introduced them. It must, however, be explained that few similar apartments are found so well furnished. Carpets are not very common in tenement-houses, and if there are any pictures, they are usually the cheapest prints. Wooden chairs, and generally every object of the cheapest, are to be met with in the dwellings of the New York poor. If we find something better in the present instance, it is not because Paul and his mother are any better off than their neighbors. On the contrary, there are few whose income is so small. But they have seen better days, and the furniture we see has been saved from the time of their comparative prosperity.

As Paul is still at his estimate, let us improve the opportunity by giving a little of their early history.

Mr. Hoffman, the father of Paul, was born in Germany, but came to New York when a boy of twelve, and there he grew up and married, his wife being an American. He was a cabinetmaker, and, being a skillful workman, earned very good wages, so that he was able to maintain his family in comfort. They occupied a neat little cottage in Harlem, and lived very happily, for Mr. Hoffman was temperate and kind, when an unfortunate accident clouded their happiness, and brought an end to their prosperity. In crossing Broadway at its most crowded part, the husband and father was run over by a loaded dray, and so seriously injured that he lived but a few hours. Then the precarious nature of their prosperity was found out. Mr. Hoffman had not saved anything, having always lived up to the extent of his income. It was obviously impossible for them to continue to live in their old home, paying a rent of twenty dollars per month. Besides, Paul did not see any good opportunity to earn his living in Harlem. So, at his instigation, his mother moved downtown, and took rooms in a tenement-house in Pearl Street, agreeing to pay six dollars a month for apartments, which would now command double the price. They brought with them furniture enough to furnish the three rooms, selling the rest for what it would bring, and thus obtaining a small reserve fund, which by this time was nearly exhausted.

Once fairly established in their new home, Paul went out into the streets to earn his living. The two most obvious, and, on the whole, most profitable trades, were blacking boots and selling newspapers. To the first Paul, who was a neat boy, objected on the score that it would keep his hands and clothing dirty, and, street boy though he had become, he had a pride in his personal appearance. To selling papers he had not the same objection, but he had a natural taste for trade, and this led him to join the ranks of the street peddlers. He began with vending matches, but found so much competition in the business, and received so rough a reception oftentimes from those who had repeated calls from others in the same business, that he gave it up, and tried something else. But the same competition which crowds the professions and the higher employments followed by men prevails among the street trades that were pursued by boys. If Paul had only had himself to support, he could have made a fair living at match selling, or any other of the employments he took up; but his mother could not earn much at making vests, and Jimmy was lame, and could do nothing to fill the common purse, so that Paul felt that his earnings must be the main support of the family, and naturally sought out what would bring him in most money.

Newsboys selling papers.

At length he had hit upon selling prize packages, and his first experience in that line is recorded in the previous chapter. Adding only that it was now a year since his father's death, we resume our narrative.

"Do you want to know how much I've made, mother?" asked Paul, looking up at length from his calculation.

"Yes, Paul."

"A dollar and thirty cents."

"I did not think it would amount to so much. The prizes came to considerable, didn't they?"

"Listen, and I will tell you how I stand:

     One pound of candy . . . . $.20
     Two packs of envelopes. . . . . . $.10
     Prize. $.90
     That makes $1.20

I sold the fifty packages at five cents each, and that brought me in two dollars and a half. Taking out the expenses, it leaves me a dollar and thirty cents. Isn't that doing well for one morning's work?"

"It's excellent; but I thought your prizes amounted to more than ninety cents."

"So they did, but several persons who bought wouldn't take their prizes, and that was so much gain."

"You have done very well, Paul. I wish you might earn as much every day."

"I'm going to earn some more this afternoon. I bought a pound of candy on the way home, and some cheap envelopes, and I'll be making up a new stock while I am waiting for dinner."

Paul took out his candy and envelopes, and set about making up the packages.

"Did any complain of the small amount of candy you put in?"

"A few; but most bought for the sake of the prizes."

"Perhaps you had better be a little more liberal with your candy, and then there may not be so much dissatisfaction where the prize is only a penny."

"I don't know but your are right, mother. I believe I'll only make thirty packages with this pound, instead of fifty. Thirty'll be all I can sell this afternoon."

Just then the door opened, and Paul's brother entered.

Jimmy Hoffman, or lame Jimmy, as he was often called, was a delicate-looking boy of ten, with a fair complexion and sweet face, but incurably lame, a defect that added to his delicate constitution, was likely to interfere seriously with his success in life. But, as frequently happens, Jimmy was all the more endeared to his mother and brother by his misfortune and bodily weakness, and if either were obliged to suffer from poverty, Jimmy would be spared the suffering.

"Well, Jimmy, have you had a pleasant walk?" asked his mother.

"Yes, mother; I went down to Fulton Market. There's a good deal to see there."

"A good deal more than in this dull room, Jimmy."

"It doesn't seem dull to me, mother, while you are here. How did you make out selling your prize packages?"

"They are all sold, Jimmy, every one. I am making some more."

"Shan't I help you?"

"Yes, I would like to have you. Just take those envelopes, and write prize packages on every one of them."

"All right, Paul," and Jimmy, glad to be of use, got the pen and ink, and, gathering up the envelopes, began to inscribe them as he had been instructed.

By the time the packages were made up, dinner was ready. It was not a very luxurious repast. There was a small piece of rump steak—not more than three-quarters of a pound—a few potatoes, a loaf of bread, and a small plate of butter. That was all; but then the cloth that covered the table was neat and clean, and the knives and forks were as bright as new, and what there was tasted good.

"What have you been doing this morning, Jimmy?" asked Paul.

"I have been drawing, Paul. Here's a picture of Friday. I copied it from 'Robinson Crusoe.'"

He showed the picture, which was wonderfully like that in the book, for this—the gift of drawing—was Jimmy's one talent, and he possessed it in no common degree.

"Excellent, Jimmy!" said Paul. "You're a real genius. I shouldn't be surprised if you'd make an artist some day."

"I wish I might," said Jimmy, earnestly. "There's nothing I'd like better."

"I'll tell you what, Jimmy. If I do well this afternoon, I'll buy you a drawing-book and some paper, to work on while mother and I are busy."

"If you can afford it, Paul, I should like it so much. Some time I might earn something that way."

"Of course you may," said Paul, cheerfully. "I won't forget you."

Dinner over, Paul went out to business, and was again successful, getting rid of his thirty packages, and clearing another dollar. Half of this he invested in a drawing-book, a pencil and some drawing-paper for Jimmy. Even then he had left of his earnings for the day one dollar and eighty cents. But this success in the new business had already excited envy and competition, as he was destined to find out on the morrow.

13

CHAPTER III

PAUL HAS COMPETITORS

The next morning Paul took his old place in front of the post office. He set down his basket in front, and, taking one of the packages in his hand, called out in a businesslike manner, as on the day before, "Here's your prize packages! Only five cents! Money prize in every package! Walk up, gentlemen, and try your luck!"

He met with a fair degree of success at first, managing in the course of an hour to sell ten packages. All the prizes drawn were small, with the exception of one ten-cent prize, which was drawn by a little bootblack, who exclaimed:

"That's the way to do business, Johnny. If you've got any more of them ten-cent prizes, I'll give you ten cents a piece for the lot."

"Better buy some more and see," said Paul.

"That don't go down," said the other. "Maybe there'd be only a penny."

A bootblack shining shoes.

Nevertheless, the effect of this large prize was to influence the sale of three other packages; but as neither of these contained more than two-cent prizes, trade began to grow dull, and for ten minutes all Paul's eloquent appeals to gentlemen to walk up and try their luck produced no effect.

At this point Paul found that there was a rival in the field.

Teddy O'Brien, who had applied for a partnership the day before, came up with a basket similar to his own, apparently filled with similar packages. He took a position about six feet distant from Paul, and began to cry out, in a shrill voice:

"Here's your bully prize packages! Best in the market! Here's where you get your big prizes, fifty cents in some of 'em. Walk up boys, tumble up, and take your pick afore they're gone. Fifty cents for five!"

"That's a lie, Teddy," said Paul, who saw that his rival's attractive announcement was likely to spoil his trade.

"No, 'tisn't," said Teddy. "If you don't believe it, just buy one and see."

"I'll tell you what I'll do," said Paul, "I'll exchange."

"No," said Teddy; "I ain't a-goin' to risk givin' fifty cents for one."

"More likely you'd get ten for one. You're a humbug."

"Have you really got any fifty-cent prizes?" asked a newsboy, who had sold out his morning stock of papers, and was lounging about the post office steps.

"Best way is to buy, Johnny," said Teddy.

The boy did buy, but his prize amounted to only one cent.

"Didn't I tell you so?" said Paul.

"Just wait a while and see," said Teddy. "The lucky feller hasn't come along. Here, Mike, jest buy a package!"

Mike, a boy of fifteen, produced five cents, and said, "I don't mind if I do."

He selected a package, and, without opening it, slipped it into his pocket.

"Why don't you open it?" said Teddy.

"What's the use?" said Mike. "There ain't no fifty cents inside."

However, he drew it out of his pocket, and opened it.

"What's this?" he exclaimed, pulling out a piece of scrip. "Howly St. Patrick! it's I that's in luck, anyhow I've got the fifty cents!"

15

And he held up to view a fifty-cent scrip.

"Let me look at it," said Paul, incredulously.

But there was no room for doubt. It was a genuine fifty cents, as Paul was compelled to admit.

"Didn't I tell you so?" said Teddy, triumphantly. "Here's where you get fifty-cent prizes."

The appeal was successful. The sight of the fifty-cent prize led to a large call for packages, of which Teddy immediately sold ten, while Paul found himself completely deserted. None of the ten, however, contained over two cents. Still the possibility of drawing fifty cents kept up the courage of buyers, while Paul's inducements were so far inferior that he found himself wholly distanced.

"Don't you wish you'd gone pardners with me?" asked Teddy, with a triumphant grin, noticing Paul's look of discomfiture. "You can't do business alongside of me."

"You can't make any money giving such big prizes," said Paul. "You haven't taken in as much as you've given yet."

"All right," said Teddy. "I'm satisfied if you are. Have a package, Jim?"

"Yes," said Jim. "Mind you give me a good prize."

The package was bought, and, on being opened, proved to contain fifty cents also, to Paul's great amazement. How Teddy's business could pay, as it was managed, he could not comprehend. One thing was certain, however, his new competitor monopolized the trade, and for two hours Paul did not get a solitary customer.

"There's something about this I don't understand," he pondered, thoughtfully. "He must lose money; but he's spoiled my trade."

Paul did not like to give up his beat, but he found himself compelled to. Accordingly he took his basket, and moved off toward Wall Street. Here he was able to start in business without competitors, and succeeded in selling quite a number of packages, until a boy came up, and said:

"There's a feller up at the post office that's givin' fifty-cent prizes. I got one of 'em."

There was a group of half-a-dozen boys around Paul, two of whom were about to invest; but on hearing thus they changed their intention, and walked off in the direction of the post office.

Looking up, Paul saw that the boy who had injured his trade was Mike, who had drawn the first fifty-cent prize from his competitor.

"Can't you stop interfering?" he said, angrily. "I've lost two customers by you."

"If you don't like it, you can lump it," said Mike, insolently. "This is a free country, ain't it?"

"It's a mean trick," said Paul, indignantly.

"Say that ag'in, and I'll upset your basket," returned Mike.

"I'll say it as often as I like," said Paul, who wasn't troubled by cowardice. "Come on, if you want to."

Mike advanced a step, doubling his fists; but, finding that Paul showed no particular sign of fear, he stopped short, saying: "I'll lick you some other time."

"You'd better put it off," said Paul. "Have a prize package, sir? Only five cents!"

This was addressed to a young man who came out of an insurance office.

"I don't mind if I do," said the young man. "Five cents, is it? What prize may I expect?"

"The highest is ten cents."

"There's a boy around the post office that gives fifty-cent prizes, mister," said Mike. "You'd better buy of him."

"I'll wait till another time," said the young man. "Here's the money, Johnny. Now for the package."

"Look here," said Paul, indignantly, when his customer had gone away; "haven't you anything to do except to drive off my customers?"

"Give me two cents on every package," said Mike, "and I'll tell 'em you give dollar prizes."

"That would be a lie, and I don't want to do business that way."

Mike continued his persecutions a while longer, and then turned the corner into Nassau Street.

"I'm glad he's gone," thought Paul. "Now there's a chance for me."

He managed after a while to sell twenty of his packages. By this time it was twelve o'clock, and he began to feel hungry. He resolved, therefore, to go home to dinner and come out again in the afternoon. He didn't know how much he had made, but probably about fifty cents. He had made more than double as much the day before in less time; but then he did not suffer from competition.

He began to doubt whether he could long pursue this business, since other competitors were likely to spring up.

As he walked by the post office he had the curiosity to look and see how his competitor was getting along.

Teddy had started, originally, with seventy-five packages; but of those scarcely a dozen were left. A group of boys were around him. Among them was Mike, who was just on the point of buying another package. As before, he put it in his pocket, and it was not till Teddy asked, "What luck, Mike?" that he drew it out, and opening it again, produced fifty cents.

"It's the big prize!" he said. "Sure I'm in luck, anyhow."

"You're the boy that's lucky," said Teddy, with a grin.

As Paul witnessed the scene a light broke upon him. Now he understood how Teddy could afford to give such large prizes. Mike and the other boy, Jim, were only confederates of his—decoy ducks—who kept drawing over again the same prize, which was eventually given back to Teddy. It was plain now why Mike put the package into his pocket before opening it. It was to exchange it for another packet into which the money had previously been placed, but which was supposed by the lookers-on to be the same that had just been purchased. The prize could afterward be placed in a new packet and used over again.

"That ain't the same package," said Paul, announcing his discovery. "He had it all the while in his pocket."

"Look here," blustered Mike, "you jest mind your own business! That's the best thing for you."

"Suppose I don't?"

"If you don't there may be a funeral to-morrow of a boy about your size."

There was a laugh at Paul's expense, but he took it coolly.

"I'll send you a particular invitation to attend, if I can get anybody to go over to the island."

18

Blackwell's island prison…referred to as "the island" several times in the book.

As Mike had been a resident at Blackwell's Island on two different occasions, this produced a laugh at his expense, in the midst of which Paul walked off.

CHAPTER IV

TEDDY GIVES UP BUSINESS

"Have you sold all your packages, Paul?" asked Jimmy, as our hero entered the humble room, where the table was already spread with a simple dinner.

"No," said Paul, "I only sold twenty. I begin to think that the prize-package business will soon be played out."

"Why?"

"There's too many that'll go into it."

Here Paul related his experience of the morning, explaining how it was that Teddy had managed to distance him in the competition.

"Can't you do the same, Paul?" asked Jimmy. "Mother's got a gold dollar she could lend you."

"That might do," said Paul; "but I don't know any boy I could trust to draw it except you, and some of them would know we were brothers."

"I think, Paul, that would be dishonest," said Mrs. Hoffman. "I would rather make less, if I were you, and do it honestly."

"Maybe you're right, mother. I'll try it again this afternoon, keeping as far away from Teddy as I can. If I find I can't make it go, I'll try some other business."

"Jimmy, have you shown Paul your drawing?" said his mother.

"Here it is, Paul," said Jimmy, producing his drawing-book, from which he had copied a simple design of a rustic cottage.

"Why, that's capital, Jimmy," said Paul, in real surprise. "I had no idea you would succeed so well."

"Do you really think so, Paul?" asked the little boy, much pleased.

"I really do. How long did it take you?"

"Only a short time—not more than half an hour, I should think," said Mrs. Hoffman. "I think Jimmy succeeded very well."

"You'll make a great artist some time, Jimmy," said Paul.

"I wish I could," said the little boy. "I should like to earn some money, so that you and mother need not work so hard."

"Hard work agrees with me. I'm tough," said Paul. "But when we get to be men, Jimmy, we'll make so much money that mother needn't work at all. She shall sit in the parlor all day, dressed in silk, with nothing to do."

"I don't think I would enjoy that," said Mrs. Hoffman, smiling.

"Will you be in the candy business, then, Paul?" said Jimmy.

"No, Jimmy. It would never do for the brother of a great artist to be selling candy round the streets. I hope I shall have something better to do than that."

"Sit down to dinner, Paul," said his mother. "It's all ready."

The dinner was not a luxurious one. There was a small plate of cold meat, some potatoes, and bread and butter; but Mrs. Hoffman felt glad to be able to provide even that, and Paul, who had the hearty appetite of a growing boy, did full justice to the fare. They had scarcely finished, when a knock was heard at the door. Paul, answering the summons, admitted a stout, pleasant-looking Irishwoman.

"The top of the mornin' to ye, Mrs. Donovan," said Paul, bowing ceremoniously.

"Ah, ye'll be afther havin' your joke, Paul," said Mrs. Donovan, good-naturedly. "And how is your health, mum, the day?"

"I am well, thank you, Mrs. Donovan," said Mrs. Hoffman. "Sit down to the table, won't you? We're just through dinner, but there's something left."

"Thank you, mum, I've jist taken dinner. I was goin' to wash this afternoon, and I thought maybe you'd have some little pieces I could wash jist as well as not."

"Thank you, Mrs. Donovan, you are very kind; but you must have enough work of your own to do."

"I'm stout and strong, mum, and hard work agrees with me; but you're a rale lady, and ain't used to it. It's only a thrifle, but if you want to pay me, you could do a bit of sewin' for me. I ain't very good with the needle. My fingers is too coarse, belike."

"Thank you, Mrs. Donovan; on those terms I will agree to your kind offer. Washing is a little hard for me."

Mrs. Hoffman collected a few pieces, and, wrapping them up in a handkerchief, handed them to her guest.

"And now what have you been doin', Jimmy darlint?" said Mrs. Donovan, turning her broad, good-humored face toward the younger boy.

"I've been drawing a picture," said Jimmy. "Would you like to see it?"

"Now, isn't that elegant?" exclaimed Mrs. Donovan, admiringly, taking the picture and gazing at it with rapt admiration. "Who showed you how to do it?"

"Paul bought me a book, and I copied it out of that."

"You're a real genius. Maybe you'll make pictures some time like them we have in the church, of the Blessed Virgin and the Saints. Do you think you could draw me, now?" she asked, with curiosity.

"I haven't got a piece of paper big enough," said Jimmy, slyly.

"Ah, it's pokin' fun at me, ye are," said Mrs. Donovan, good-humoredly. "Just like my Pat; he run into the room yesterday sayin', 'Mother, there's great news. Barnum's fat woman is dead, and he's comin' afther you this afternoon. He'll pay you ten dollars a week and board.' 'Whist, ye spalpeen!' said I; 'is it makin' fun of your poor mother, ye are?' but I couldn't help laughing at the impertinence of the boy. But I must be goin'."

"Thank you for your kind offer, Mrs. Donovan. Jimmy shall go to your room for the sewing."

"There's no hurry about that," said Mrs. Donovan. "I'll jist bring it in meself when it's ready."

"She is very kind," said Mrs. Hoffman, when Bridget Donovan had gone. "I shall be glad to have her wash. I am apt to feel weak after it. What are you going to do this afternoon, Paul?"

"I'll try to sell out the rest of my stock of packages. Perhaps I shan't succeed, but I'll do my best. Shall you have another picture to show me when I come back tonight, Jimmy?"

"Yes, Paul; I love to draw. I'm going to try this castle."

"It's rather hard, isn't it?"

"I can do it," said Jimmy, confidently.

Paul left the room with his basket on his arm.

He was drawn by curiosity to the spot where he had met with his first success, as well as his first failure—the front of the post office. Here he became witness to an unexpectedly lively scene; in other words, a fight, in which Teddy O'Brien and his confederate, Mike, were the contestants. To explain the cause of the quarrel, it must be stated that it related to a division of the spoils.

Teddy had sold out his last package, seventy-five in number. For these he had received five cents apiece, making in all three dollars and seventy-five cents, of which all but a dollar and seventy-five cents, representing the value of the prizes and the original cost of the packages and their contents, was profit. Now, according to the arrangement entered into between him and Mike, the latter, for his services, was to receive one cent on every package sold. This, however, seemed to Teddy too much to pay, so, when the time of reckoning came, he stoutly asseverated that there were but sixty packages.

"That don't go down," said Mike, indignantly; "it's nearer a hundred."

"No, it isn't. It's only sixty. You've got the fifty cents, and I'll give you ten more."

"You must give me the whole sixty, then," said Mike, changing his ground. "I drawed the fifty as a prize."

Teddy was struck with astonishment at the impudence of this assumption.

"It wasn't no prize," he said.

"Yes, it was," said Mike. "You said so yourself. Didn't he, Jim?"

Jim, who was also a confederate, but had agreed to accept twenty-five cents in full for services rendered, promptly answered:

"Shure, Mike's right. It was a prize he drew."

"You want to chate me!" said Teddy, angrily.

"What have you been doin' all the mornin'?" demanded Mike. "You're the chap to talk about chatin', ain't you?"

"I'll give you twenty-five cents," said Teddy, "and that's all I will give you."

"Then you've got to fight," said Mike, squaring off.

"Yes, you've got to fight!" chimed in Jim, who thought he saw a chance for more money.

Teddy looked at his two enemies, each of whom was probably more than a match for himself, and was not long in deciding that his best course was to avoid a fight by running. Accordingly, he tucked all the money into his pocket, and, turning incontinently, fled down Liberty Street, closely pursued by his late confederates. Paul came up just in time to hear the termination of the dispute and watch the flight of his late business rival.

"I guess Teddy won't go into the business again," he reflected. "I may as well take my old stand."

Accordingly he once more installed himself on the post office steps, and began to cry, "Prize packages. Only five cents!"

23

Having no competitor now to interfere with his trade, he met with fair success, and by four o'clock was able to start for home with his empty basket, having disposed of all his stock in trade.

His profits, though not so great as the day before, amounted to a dollar.

"If I could only make a dollar every day," thought Paul, "I would be satisfied."

CHAPTER V

PAUL LOSES HIS BASKET

Paul continued in the prize-package business for three weeks. His success varied, but he never made less than seventy-five cents a day, and sometimes as much as a dollar and a quarter. He was not without competitors. More than once, on reaching his accustomed stand, he found a rival occupying it before him. In such cases he quietly passed on, and set up his business elsewhere, preferring to monopolize the trade, though the location might not be so good.

Teddy O'Brien did not again enter the field. We left him, at the end of the last chapter, trying to escape from Mike and Jim, who demanded a larger sum than he was willing to pay for their services. He succeeded in escaping with his money, but the next day the two confederates caught him, and Teddy received a black eye as a receipt in full of all demands. So, on the whole, he decided that some other business would suit him better, and resumed the blacking-box, which he had abandoned on embarking in commercial pursuits.

Mike Donovan and Jim Parker were two notoriously bad boys, preferring to make a living in any other way than by honest industry. As some of these ways were not regarded as honest in the sight of the law, each had more than once been sentenced to a term at Blackwell's Island. They made a proposition to Paul to act as decoy ducks for him in the same way as for Teddy. He liked neither of the boys, and did not care to be associated with them. This refusal Mike and Jim resented, and determined to "pay off" Paul if they ever got a chance. Our hero from time to time saw them hovering about him, but took very little notice of them.

He knew that he was a match for either, though Mike exceeded him in size, and he felt quite capable of taking care of himself.

One day Mike and Jim, whose kindred tastes led them to keep company, met at the corner of Liberty and William streets. Mike looked unusually dilapidated. He had had a scuffle the day before with another boy, and his clothes, always well ventilated, got torn in several extra places. As it was very uncertain when he would be in a financial condition to provide himself with another suit, the prospect was rather alarming. Jim Parker looked a shade more respectable in attire, but his face and hands were streaked with blacking. To this, however, Jim had become so accustomed that he would probably have felt uncomfortable with a clean face.

"How are you off for stamps, Jim?" asked Mike.

"Dead broke," was the reply.

"So am I. I ain't had no breakfast."

"Nor I 'cept an apple. Couldn't I eat, though?"

"Suppose we borrow a quarter of Paul Hoffman."

"He wouldn't lend a feller."

"Not if he knowed it," said Mike, significantly.

"What do you mean, Mike?" asked Jim, with some curiosity.

"We'll borrow without leave."

"How'll we do it?"

"I'll tell you," said Mike.

He proceeded to unfold his plan, which was briefly this. The two were to saunter up to where Paul was standing; and remain until the group, if there were any around him, should be dispersed. Then one was to pull his hat over his eyes, while the other would snatch the basket containing his prize packages, and run down Liberty Street, never stopping until he landed in a certain alley known to both boys. The other would run in a different direction, and both would meet as soon as practicable for the division of the spoils. It was yet so early that Paul could not have sold many from his stock. As each contained a prize, varying from one penny to ten, they would probably realize enough to buy a good breakfast, besides the candy contained in the packages. More money might be obtained by selling packages, but there was risk in this. Besides, it would take time, and they decided that a bird in the hand was worth two in the bush.

"That's a good idea," said Jim, approvingly. "Who'll knock his hat over his head?"

"You can," said Mike, "and I'll grab the basket." But to this Jim demurred, for two reasons: first, he was rather afraid of Paul, whose strength of arm he had tested on a previous occasion; and, again, he was afraid that if Mike got off with the basket he would appropriate the lion's share.

"I'll grab the basket," he said.

"What for?" said Mike, suspiciously, for he, too, felt some distrust of his confederate.

"You're stronger'n I am, Mike," said Jim. "Maybe he'd turn on me, and I can't fight him as well as you."

"That's so," said Mike, who had rather a high idea of his own prowess, and felt pleased with the compliment. "I'm a match for him."

"Of course you be," said Jim, artfully, "and he knows it."

"Of course he does," said Mike, boastfully. "I can lick him with one hand."

Jim had serious doubts of this, but he had his reasons for concurring in Mike's estimate of his own powers.

"We'd better start now," said Jim. "I'm awful hungry."

"Come along, then."

They walked up Liberty Street, as far as Nassau. On reaching the corner they saw their unconscious victim at his usual place. It was rather a public place for an assault, and both boys would have hesitated had they not been incited by a double motive—the desire of gain and a feeling of hostility.

They sauntered along, and Mike pressed in close by Paul.

"What do you want?" asked Paul, not liking the vicinity.

"What's that to you?" demanded Mike.

"Quit crowdin' me."

"I ain't crowdin'. I've got as much right to be here as you."

"Here's your prize packages!" exclaimed Paul, in a businesslike tone.

"Maybe I'll buy one if you'll give me credit till to-morrow," said Mike.

"Your credit isn't good with me," said Paul. "You must pay cash down."

"Then you won't trust me?" said Mike, pressing a little closer.

"No, I won't," said Paul, decidedly.

"Then, take that, you spalpeen!" said Mike, suddenly pulling Paul's hat over his eyes.

At the same time Jim, to whom he had tipped a wink, snatched the basket, which Paul held loosely in his hand, and disappeared round the corner.

The attack was so sudden and unexpected that Paul was at first bewildered. But he quickly recovered his presence of mind, and saw into the trick. He raised his hat, and darted in pursuit of Mike, not knowing in what direction his basket had gone.

———

27

"That's a mean trick!" he exclaimed, indignantly. "Give me back my basket, you thief!"

"I ain't got no basket," said Mike, facing round.

"Then you know where it is."

"I don't know nothin' of your basket."

"You pulled my hat over my eyes on purpose to steal my basket."

"No, I didn't. You insulted me, that's why I did it."

"Tell me where my basket is, or I'll lick you," said Paul, incensed.

"I ain't nothin' to do with your basket."

"Take that, then, for pulling my hat over my eyes," and Paul, suiting the action to the word, dealt Mike a staggering blow in the face.

"I'll murder you!" shouted Mike, furiously, dashing at Paul with a blow which might have leveled him, if he had not fended it off.

Paul was not quarrelsome, but he knew how to fight, and he was prepared now to fight in earnest, indignant as he was at the robbery which entailed upon him a loss he could ill sustain.

"I'll give you all you want," he said, resolutely, eyeing Mike warily, and watching a chance to give him another blow.

The contest was brief, being terminated by the sudden and unwelcome arrival of a policeman.

"What's this?" he asked authoritatively, surveying the combatants; Paul, with his flushed face, and Mike, whose nose was bleeding freely from a successful blow of his adversary.

"He pitched into me for nothin'," said Mike, glaring at Paul, and rubbing his bloody nose on the sleeve of his ragged coat.

"That isn't true," said Paul, excitedly. "He came up while I was selling prize packages of candy in front of the post office, and pulled my hat over my eyes, while another boy grabbed my basket."

"You lie!" said Mike. "I don't know nothin' of your basket."

"Why did you pull his hat over his eyes?" asked the policeman.

"Because he insulted me."

"How did he insult you?"

"He wouldn't trust me till to-morrow."

"I don't blame him much for that," said the policeman, who was aware of Mike's shady reputation, having on a former occasion been under the necessity of arresting him. Even without such

---

acquaintance, Mike's general appearance would hardly have recommended him to Officer Jones.

"I'll let you go this time," he said, "but if I catch you fighting again on my beat I'll march you off to the station-house."

Mike was glad to escape, though he would almost have been willing to be arrested if Paul could have been arrested also.

The officer walked away, and Mike started down the street.

Paul followed him.

That didn't suit Mike's ideas, as he was anxious to meet Jim and divide the spoils with him.

"What are you follerin' me for?" he demanded, angrily.`

"I have my reasons," said Paul.

"Then you'd better stay where you are. Your company ain't wanted."

"I know that," said Paul, "but I'm going to follow you till I find my basket."

"What do I know of your basket?"

"That's what I want to find out."

Mike saw, by Paul's resolute tone, that he meant what he said. Desirous of shaking him of, he started on a run.

CHAPTER VI

PAUL AS AN ARTIST

Paul was not slow in following Mike. He was a good runner, and would have had no difficulty in keeping up with his enemy if the streets had been empty. But to thread his way in and out among the numerous foot passengers that thronged the sidewalks was not so easy. He kept up pretty well, however, until, in turning a street corner, he ran at full speed into a very stout gentleman, whose scanty wind was quite knocked out of him by the collision. He glared in anger at Paul, but could not at first obtain breath enough to speak.

"I beg your pardon, sir," said Paul, who, in spite of his desire to overtake Mike, felt it incumbent upon him to stop and offer an apology.

"What do you mean, sir," exploded the fat man, at last, "by tearing through the streets like a locomotive? You've nearly killed me."

"I am very sorry, sir."

"You ought to be. Don't you know better than to run at such speed? You ought to be indicted as a public nuisance.

"I was trying to catch a thief," said Paul.

"Trying to catch a thief? How's that?" asked the stout gentleman, his indignation giving way to curiosity.

"I was selling packages in front of the post office when he and another boy came up and stole my basket."

"Indeed! What were you selling?"

"Prize packages, sir."

"What was in them?"

"Candy."

"Could you make much that way?"

About a dollar a day."

"I'd rather have given you a dollar than had you run against me with such violence. I feel it yet."

"Indeed, sir, I'm very sorry."

"Well, I'll forgive you, under the circumstances. What's your name?"

"Paul Hoffman."

"Well, I hope you'll get back your basket. Some time, if you see me in the street, come up and let me know. Would you know me again?"

"I think I should, sir."

"Well, good-morning. I hope you'll catch the thief."

"I thank you, sir."

They parted company, but Paul did not continue the pursuit. The conversation in which he had taken part had lasted so long that Mike had had plenty of time to find a refuge, and there would be no use in following him.

So Paul went home.

"You are home early, Paul," said his mother. "Surely you haven't sold out by this time."

"No, but all my packages are gone."

"How is that?"

"They were stolen."

"Tell me about it."

So Paul told the story.

"That Mike was awful mean," said Jimmy, indignantly. "I'd like to hit him."

"I don't think you would hurt him much, Jimmy," said Paul, amused at his little brother's vehemence.

"Then I wish I was a big, strong boy," said Jimmy.

"I hope you will be, some time."

"How much was your loss, Paul?" asked his mother.

"There were nearly forty packages. They cost me about a dollar, but if I had sold them all they would have brought me in twice as much. I had only sold ten packages."

"Shall you make some more?"

"No, I think not," said Paul. "I've got tired of the business. It's getting poorer every day. I'll go out after dinner, and see if I can't find something else to do."

"You ain't going out now, Paul?" said Jimmy.

"No, I'll stop and see you draw a little while."

"That's bully. I'm going to try these oxen."

"That's a hard picture. I don't think you can draw it, Jimmy."

"Yes, I can," said the little boy, confidently. "Just see if I don't."

"Jimmy has improved a good deal," said his mother.

"You'll be a great artist one of these days, Jimmy," said Paul.

"I'm going to try, Paul," said the little boy. "I like it so much."

Little Jimmy had indeed made surprising progress in drawing. With no instruction whatever, he had succeeded in a very close and accurate imitation of the sketches in the drawing books Paul had purchased for him. It was a great delight to the little boy to draw, and hour after hour, as his mother sat at her work, he sat up to the table, and worked at his drawing, scarcely speaking a word unless spoken to, so absorbed was he in his fascinating employment.

Paul watched him attentively.

"You'll make a bully artist, Jimmy," he said, at length, really surprised at his little brother's proficiency. "If you keep on a little longer, you'll beat me."

"I wish you'd draw something, Paul," said Jimmy. "I never saw any of your drawings."

"I am afraid, if you saw mine, it would discourage you," said Paul. "You know, I'm older and ought to draw better."

His face was serious, but there was a merry twinkle of fun in his eyes.

"Of course, I know you draw better," said Jimmy, seriously.

"What shall I draw?" asked Paul.

"Try this horse, Paul."

"All right!" said Paul. "But you must go away; I don't want you to see it till it is done."

Jimmy left the table, and Paul commenced his attempt. Now, though Paul is the hero of my story, I am bound to confess that he had not the slightest talent for drawing, though Jimmy did not know it. It was only to afford his little brother amusement that he now undertook the task.

Paul worked away for about five minutes.

"It's done," he said.

"So quick?" exclaimed Jimmy, in surprise. "How fast you work!"

He drew near and inspected Paul's drawing. He had no sooner inspected it than he burst into a fit of laughter. Paul's drawing was a very rough one, and such a horse as he had drawn will never probably be seen until the race has greatly degenerated.

"What's the matter, Jimmy?" asked Paul. "Don't you like it?"

"It's awful, Paul," said the little boy, almost choking with mirth.

"I see how it is," said Paul, with feigned resentment. "You're jealous of me because you can't draw as well."

"Oh, Paul, you'll kill me!" and Jimmy again burst into a fit of merriment. "Can't you really draw any better?"

"No, Jimmy," said Paul, joining in the laugh. "I can't draw any better than an old cow. You've got all the talent in the family in that line."

"But you're smart in other ways, Paul," said Jimmy, who had a great admiration of Paul, notwithstanding the discovery of his artistic inferiority.

"I'm glad there's one that thinks so, Jimmy," said Paul. "I'll refer to you when I want a recommendation."

Jimmy resumed his drawing, and was proud of the praises which Paul freely bestowed upon him.

"I'll get you a harder drawing book when you've got through with these," said Paul; "that is, if I don't get reduced to poverty by having my stock in trade stolen again."

After a while came dinner. This meal in Mrs. Hoffman's household usually came at twelve o'clock. It was a plain, frugal meal always, but on Sunday they usually managed to have something a little better, as they had been accustomed to do when Mr. Hoffman was alive.

Paul was soon through.

He took his hat from the bureau, and prepared to go out.

"I'm going out to try my luck, mother," he said. "I'll see if I can't get into something I like a little better than the prize-package business."

"I hope you'll succeed, Paul."

"Better than I did in drawing horses, eh, Jimmy?"

"Yes, I hope so, Paul," said the little boy.

"Don't you show that horse to visitors and pretend it's yours, Jimmy."

"No danger, Paul."

Paul went downstairs and into the street. He had no definite plan in his head, but was ready for anything that might turn up. He did not feel anxious, for he knew there were plenty of ways in which he could earn something. He had never tried blacking boots, but still he could do it in case of emergency. He had sold papers, and succeeded fairly in that line, and knew he could again. He had pitted himself against other boys, and the result had been to give him a certain confidence in his own powers and business abilities. When he had

---

33

first gone into the street to try his chances there, it had been with a degree of diffidence. But knocking about the streets soon gives a boy confidence, sometimes too much of it; and Paul had learned to rely upon himself; but the influence of a good, though humble home, and a judicious mother, had kept him aloof from the bad habits into which many street boys are led.

So Paul, though his stock in trade had been stolen, and he was obliged to seek a new kind of business, was by no means disheartened. He walked a little way downtown, and then, crossing the City Hall Park, found himself on Broadway.

A little below the Astor House he came to the stand of a sidewalk-merchant, who dealt in neckties. Upon an upright framework hung a great variety of ties of different colors, most of which were sold at the uniform price of twenty-five cents each.

Paul was acquainted with the proprietor of the stand, and, having nothing else to do, determined to stop and speak to him.

CHAPTER VII

A NEW BUSINESS

The proprietor of the necktie stand was a slender, dark-complexioned young man of about twenty-five, or thereabouts.

His name was George Barry. Paul had known him for over a year, and whenever he passed, his stand was accustomed to stop and speak with him.

"Well, George, how's business?" asked Paul.

"Fair," said Barry. "That isn't what's the matter."

"What is it, then?"

"I'm sick. I ought not to be out here to-day."

"What's the matter with you?"

"I've caught a bad cold, and feel hot and feverish. I ought to be at home and abed."

"Why don't you go?"

"I can't leave my business."

"It's better to do that than to get a bad sickness."

"I suppose it is. I am afraid I am going to have a fever. One minute I'm hot, another I'm cold. But I can't afford to close up my business."

"Why don't you get somebody to take your place?"

"I don't know anybody I could get that I could trust. They'd sell my goods, and make off with the money."

"Can you trust me?" asked Paul, who saw a chance to benefit himself as well as his friend.

"Yes, Paul, I could trust you, but I'm afraid I couldn't pay you enough to make it worth while for you to stand here."

"I haven't got anything to do just now," said Paul. "I was in the prize-package business, but two fellows stole my stock in trade, and I'm not going into it again. It's about played out. I'm your man. Just make me an offer."

"I should like to have you take my place for a day or two, for I know you wouldn't cheat me."

"You may be sure of that."

"I am sure. I know you are an honest boy, Paul. But I don't know what to offer you."

"How many neckties do you sell a day?" asked Paul, in a businesslike tone.

"About a dozen on an average."

"And how much profit do you make?"

"It's half profit."

Paul made a short calculation. Twelve neckties at twenty-five cents each would bring three dollars. Half of this was a dollar and a half.

"I'll take your place for half profits," he said.

"That's fair," said George Barry. "I'll accept your offer. Can you begin now?"

"Yes."

"Then I'll go home and go to bed. It's the best place for me."

"You'd better. I'll come round after closing up, and hand over the money."

"All right! You know where I live?"

"I'm not sure."

"No. — Bleecker street."

"I'll come up this evening."

George Barry walked away, leaving Paul in charge of his business.

He did so with perfect confidence. Not every boy in Paul's circumstances can be trusted, but he felt sure that Paul would do the right thing by him.

I may as well say, in this connection, that George Barry had a mother living. They occupied two rooms in a lodging-house in Bleecker street, and lived very comfortably. Mrs. Barry had an allowance of two hundred dollars a year from a relation. This, with what she earned by sewing, and her son by his stand, supported them very comfortably, especially as they provided and cooked their own food, which was, of course, much cheaper than boarding. Still, the loss of the young man's earnings, even for a short time, would have been felt, though they had a reserve of a hundred dollars in a savings bank, from which they might draw if necessary. But George did not like to do this. The arrangement which he made with Paul was a satisfactory one, for with half his usual earnings they would still be able to keep out of debt, and not be compelled to draw upon the fund in the bank. Of course, something depended on Paul's success as a salesman, but he would not be likely to fall much below the average amount of sales. So, on the whole, George Barry went home considerably relieved in mind, though his head was throbbing, and he felt decidedly sick.

Arrived at home, his mother, who understood sickness, at once took measures to relieve him.

"Don't mind the loss of a few days, George," she said, cheerfully; "we shall be able to get along very well."

"It'll only be part loss, mother," he said. "I've got Paul Hoffman to take my place for half the profits."

"Paul Hoffman! Do I know him?"

"I don't think he has ever been here but I have known him for a year."

"Can you trust him?"

"Yes, I'm not at all afraid. He is a smart boy, and as honest as he is smart. I think he will sell nearly as much as I would."

"That is an excellent arrangement. You needn't feel uneasy, then."

"No, the business will go on right."

"I should like to see your salesman."

"You'll see him to-night, mother. He's coming round this evening to let me know how he's got along, and hand over the money he's taken."

"You'd better be quiet now, George, and go to sleep, if you can. I'll make you some warm tea. I think it'll do you good."

Meanwhile Paul assumed charge of George Barry's business. He was sorry his friend was sick, but he congratulated himself on getting into business so soon.

"It's more respectable than selling prize packages," thought Paul. "I wish I had a stand of my own."

He was still a street merchant, but among street merchants there are grades as well as among merchants whose claim to higher respectability rests upon having rent to pay. Paul felt that it was almost like having a shop of his own. He had always looked up to George Barry as standing higher than himself in a business way, and he felt that even if his earnings should not be as great, that it was a step upward to have sole charge of his stand, if only for a day or two.

Paul's ambition was aroused. It was for his interest to make as large sales as possible. Besides, he thought he would like to prove to George Barry that he had made a good selection in appointing him his substitute.

37

Now, if the truth must be told, George Barry himself was not possessed of superior business ability. He was lacking in energy and push. He could sell neckties to those who asked for them, but had no particular talent for attracting trade. He would have been a fair clerk, but was never likely to rise above a very moderate success. Paul was quite different. He was quick, enterprising, and smart. He was a boy likely to push his way to success unless circumstances were very much against him.

"I'd like to sell more than George Barry," he said to himself. "I don't know if I can, but I'm going to try."

The day was half over, and probably the most profitable, so far as business was concerned. Paul had only four or five hours left.

"Let me see," he said to himself. "I ought to sell six neckties to come up to the average of half a day's sale. I wonder whether I can do it."

As his soliloquy ended, his quick eye detected a young man glancing at his stock, and he observed that he paused irresolutely, as if half inclined to purchase.

"Can't I sell you a necktie to-day?" asked Paul, promptly.

"I don't know," said the other. "What do you charge?"

"You can have your choice for twenty-five cents. That is cheap, isn't it?"

"Yes, that's cheap. Let me look at them."

"Here's one that will suit your complexion," said Paul.

"Yes, that's a pretty one. I think I'll take it."

"You have to pay twice as much in the shops," continued Paul, as he rolled it up. "You see, we have no rent to pay, and so we can sell cheap. You'll save money by always buying your neckties here."

"The only objection to that is that I don't live in the city. I am here only for a day. I live about fifty miles in the country."

"Then I'll tell you what you'd better do," said Paul. "Lay in half a dozen, while you are about it. It'll only be a dollar and a half, and you'll save as much as that by doing it."

"I don't know but you are right," said his customer, whom the suggestion impressed favorably. "As you say, it's only a dollar and a half, and it'll give me a good stock."

"Let me pick them out for you," said Paul, briskly, "unless there's something you see yourself."

"I like that one."

"All right. What shall be the next?"

Finally, the young man selected the entire half-dozen, and deposited a dollar and a half in Paul's hands.

"Come and see me again," said Paul, "and if you have any friends coming to the city, send them to me."

"I will," said the other.

"Tell them it's the first stand south of the Astor House. Then they won't miss it."

"That's a good beginning," said Paul to himself, with satisfaction. "Half a day's average sales already, and I've only been here fifteen minutes. Let me see, what will my profits be on that? Three shillings, I declare. That isn't bad, now!"

Paul had reason to be satisfied with himself. If he had not spoken, the young man would very probably have gone on without purchasing at all, or, at any rate, remained content with a single necktie. Paul's manner and timely word had increased his purchase sixfold. That is generally the difference between a poor salesman and one of the first class. Anybody can sell to those who are anxious to buy; but it takes a smart man to persuade a customer that he wants what otherwise he would go without. The difference in success is generally appreciated by dealers, and a superior salesman is generally paid a handsome salary.

"I don't believe George Barry would have sold that man so many ties," thought Paul. "I hope I shall have as good luck next time."

But this, of course, was not to be expected. It is not every customer who can be persuaded to buy half-a-dozen ties, even by the most eloquent salesman. However, in the course of an hour more, Paul had sold three more to single customers. Then came a man who bought two. Then there was a lull, and for an hour Paul sold none at all. But business improved a little toward the close of the afternoon, and when it was time to close up, our young merchant found that he had disposed of fifteen.

My share of the profits will be ninety-three cents," thought Paul, with satisfaction. "That isn't bad for an afternoon's work."

CHAPTER VIII

A STROKE OF ILL LUCK

Paul transferred his frame of goods to a neighboring office at the end of the afternoon, the arrangement having been made by George Barry, on first entering into business as a street merchant. This saved a good deal of trouble, as otherwise he would have been compelled to carry them home every night and bring them back in the morning.

"Well, Paul," asked his mother, when he returned to supper, "have you found anything to do yet?"

"I have got employment for a few days," said Paul, "to tend a necktie stand. The man that keeps it is sick."

"How much does he pay you, Paul?" asked Jimmy.

"Half the profits. How much do you think I have made this afternoon?"

"Forty cents."

"What do you say to ninety-three cents? Just look at this," and Paul displayed his earnings.

"That is excellent."

"I had good luck. Generally, I shan't make more in a whole day than this."

"That will be doing very well."

"But I shall make more, if I can. One fellow bought six neckties of me this afternoon. I wish everybody would do that. Now, mother, I hope supper is most ready, for selling neckties has made me hungry."

"Almost ready, Paul."

It was a humble meal, but a good one. There were fresh rolls and butter, tea and some cold meat. That was all; but the cloth was clean, and everything looked neat. All did justice to the plain meal, and never thought of envying the thousands who, in their rich uptown mansions, were sitting down at the same hour to elaborate dinners costing more than their entire week's board.

"Are you going out, Paul?" asked Mrs. Hoffman, noticing that he took his hat.

"Yes, I must go and see George Barry, and carry the money I have received for sales."

"Where does he live?"

"In Bleecker Street. I shan't be gone long."

Paul reached the number which had been given him. It was a large, four-story house, with the appearance of a barracks.

"Mr. Barry," said the servant, in answer to his question—"he lives upstairs on the fourth floor. Room on the right."

Paul plodded his way upstairs, and found the room without difficulty.

On knocking, the door was opened by Mrs. Barry, who looked at him inquiringly.

"Does George Barry live here?" asked Paul.

"Yes. Are you the one he left in charge of his business?"

Paul answered in the affirmative, adding, "How is he?"

"He seems quite feverish. I am afraid he is going to have a fever. It's fortunate he came home. He was not able to attend to his business."

"Can I see him?"

"Come in," said Mrs. Barry.

The room was covered with a worn carpet, but looked neat and comfortable. There was a cheap sewing machine in one corner, and some plain furniture. There was a bedroom opening out of this room, and here it was that George Barry lay upon the bed.

"Is that Paul Hoffman, mother?" was heard from the bedroom.

"Yes," said Paul, answering for himself.

"Go in, if you like," said Mrs. Barry. "My son wishes to see you.

"How do you feel now, George?" asked Paul.

"Not very well, Paul. I didn't give up a minute too soon. I think I am going to have a fever."

"That is not comfortable," said Paul. "Still, you have your mother to take care of you."

"I don't know how I should get along without her. Can you look after my business as long as I am sick?"

"Yes; I have nothing else to do."

"Then that is off my mind. By the way, how many ties did you sell this afternoon?"

"Fifteen."

"What!" demanded Barry, in surprise. "You sold fifteen?"

"Yes."

"Why, I never sold so many as that in an afternoon."

"Didn't you?" said Paul, gratified. "Then you think I did well?"

—

"Splendidly. How did you do it?"

"You see, there was a young man from the country that I persuaded to buy six, as he could not get them so cheap at home. That was my first sale, and it encouraged me."

"I didn't think you'd sell more than six in the whole afternoon."

"Nor did I, when I started; but I determined to do my best. I don't expect to do as well every day."

"No, of course not. I've been in the business more than a year; and I know what it is. Some days are very dull."

"I've got the money for you. The fifteen ties came to three dollars and seventy-five cents. I keep one-fourth of this as my commission. That leaves two dollars and eighty-two cents."

"Quite correct. However, you needn't give me the money. You may need to change a bill, or else lose a sale. It will do if you settle with me at the end of the week."

"I see you have confidence in me, George. Suppose I should take a fancy to run away with the money?"

"I am not afraid."

"If I do, I will give you warning a week beforehand."

After a little more conversation, Paul withdrew, thinking he might worry the sick man. He offered to come up the next evening, but George Barry said, "It would be too much to expect you to come up every evening. I shall be satisfied if you come up every other evening."

"Very well," said Paul. "Then you may expect me Saturday. I hope I shall have some good sales to report, and that I shall find you better."

Paul descended to the street, and walked slowly homeward. He couldn't help wishing that the stand was his own, and the entire profits his. This would double his income, and enable him to save up money. At present this was hardly possible. His own earnings had been, and were likely to continue being, very fluctuating.

Still, they constituted the main support of the family. His mother made shirts for an establishment on Broadway at twenty-five cents each, which was more than some establishments paid. She could hardly average more than one shirt a day, in addition to her household work, and in order to accomplish this, even, she was obliged to work very steadily all day. Jimmy, of course, earned nothing. Not that he was too young. There were plenty of little newsboys who were as small as he—perhaps smaller. I have seen boys, who did not appear to be more than four years old, standing at the corners, crying the news in their childish treble. But Paul was not willing to have Jimmy sent out into the streets to undergo the rough discipline of street life. He was himself of a strong, robust nature, and did not shrink from the rough and tumble of life. He felt sure he could make his way, and give as well as receive blows. But Jimmy was shy and retiring, of a timid, shrinking nature, who would suffer from what would only exhilarate Paul, and brace him for the contest. So it was understood that Jimmy was to get an education, studying at present at home with his mother, who had received a good education, and that Mrs. Hoffman and Paul were to be the breadwinners. "I wish mother didn't have to sit so steadily at her work," thought Paul, many a time. He resolved some time to relieve her from the necessity; but at present it was impossible.

To maintain their small family in comfort required all that both could earn.

The next morning Paul started out after breakfast for the street stand, wondering what success he was destined to meet with.

About the middle of the forenoon Mrs. Hoffman prepared to go out.

"Do you think you can stay alone for an hour or two, Jimmy?" she asked.

"Yes, mother," answered Jimmy, who was deep in a picture which he was copying from one of the drawing-books Paul had bought him. "Where are you going, mother?"

"To carry back some work, Jimmy. I have got half-a-dozen shirts done, and must return them, and ask for more."

"They ought to pay you more than twenty-five cents apiece, mother. How long has it taken you to make them?"

"Nearly a week."

"That is only a dollar and a half for a week's work."

"I know it, Jimmy; but they can get plenty to work at that price, so it won't do for me to complain. I shall be very glad if I can get steady work, even at that price."

Jimmy said no more, and Mrs. Hoffman, gathering up her bundle, went out.

She had a little more than half a mile to go. This did not require long. She entered the large door, and advanced to the counter behind which stood a clerk with a pen behind his ear.

"How many?" he said, as she laid the bundle upon the counter.

"Six."

"Name?"

"Hoffman."

"Correct. I will look at them."

He opened the bundle hastily, and surveyed the work critically. Luckily there was no fault to find, for Mrs. Hoffman was a skillful seamstress.

"They will do," he said, and, taking from a drawer the stipulated sum, paid for them.

"Can I have some more?" asked Mrs. Hoffman, anxiously.

"Not to-day. We're overstocked with goods made up. We must contract our manufacture."

This was unexpected, and carried dismay to the heart of the poor woman. What she could earn was very little but it was important to her.

"When do you think you can give me some more work?" she asked.

"It may be a month or six weeks," he answered, carelessly.

A month or six weeks! To have her supply of work cut off for so long a time would, indeed, be a dire misfortune. But there was nothing to say. Mrs. Hoffman knew very well that no one in the establishment cared for her necessities. So, with a heavy heart, she started for home, making up her mind to look elsewhere for work in the afternoon. She could not help recalling, with sorrow, the time when her husband was living, and they lived in a pleasant little home, before the shadow of bereavement and pecuniary anxiety had come to cloud their happiness. Still, she was not utterly cast down. Paul had proved himself a manly and a helpful boy, self-reliant and courageous, and, though they might be pinched, she knew that as long as he was able to work they would not actually suffer.

CHAPTER IX

A NEW PATRON

Mrs. Hoffman went out in the afternoon, and visited several large establishments in the hope of obtaining work. But everywhere she was met with the stereotyped reply, "Business is so dull that we are obliged to turn off some who are accustomed to work for us. We have no room for new hands."

Finally she decided that it would be of no use to make any further applications, and went home, feeling considerably disheartened.

"I must find something to do," she said to herself. "I cannot throw upon Paul the entire burden of supporting the family."

But it was not easy to decide what to do. There are so few paths open to a woman like Mrs. Hoffman. She was not strong enough to take in washing, nor, if she had been, would Paul, who was proud for his mother, though not for himself, have consented to her doing it. She determined to think it over during the evening, and make another attempt to get work of some kind the next day.

"I won't tell Paul till tomorrow night," she decided. "Perhaps by that time I shall have found something to do."

All that day, the first full day in his new business, Paul sold eighteen ties. He was not as successful proportionately as the previous afternoon. Still his share of the profits amounted to a dollar and twelve cents, and he felt quite satisfied. His sales had been fifty per cent more than George Barry's average sales, and that was doing remarkably well, considering that the business was a new one to him.

The next morning about ten o'clock, as he stood behind his stand, he saw a stout gentleman approaching from the direction of the Astor House. He remembered him as the one with whom he had accidentally come in collision when he was in pursuit of Mike Donovan. Having been invited to speak to him, he determined to do so.

"Good-morning, sir," said Paul, politely.

"Eh? Did you speak to me?" inquired the stout gentleman.

"Yes, sir; I bade you good-morning."

"Good-morning. I don't remember you, though. What's your name?"

"Paul Hoffman. Don't you remember my running against you a day or two since?"

"Oho! You're the boy, then. You nearly knocked the breath out of me."

"I am very sorry, sir."

"Of course you didn't mean to. Is this your stand?"

"No, sir; I am tending for the owner, who is sick."

"Does he pay you well?"

"He gives me half the profits."

"And does that pay you for your labor?"

"I can earn about a dollar a day."

"That is good. It is more than I earned when I was of your age."

"Indeed, sir!"

"Yes; I was a poor boy, but I kept steadily at work, and now I am rich."

"I hope I shall be rich some time," said Paul.

"You have the same chance that I had."

"I don't care so much for myself as for my mother and my little brother. I should like to become rich for their sake."

"So you have a mother and a brother. Where do they live?"

Paul told him.

"And you help support them?"

"Yes, sir."

"That's a good boy," said the gentleman, approvingly. "Is your mother able to earn anything?"

"Not much, sir. She makes shirts for a Broadway store, but they only pay her twenty-five cents apiece."

"That's very small. She can sew well, I suppose?"

"Oh, yes, sir; no fault is ever found with her work."

"Do you think she would make me a dozen shirts?"

"She would be glad to do so," said Paul, quickly, for he knew that his new acquaintance would pay far more liberally than the Broadway firm.

"I will give the price I usually pay—ten shillings apiece."

Ten shillings in New York currency amount to a dollar and a quarter, which would be five times the price Mrs. Hoffman had been accustomed to receive. A dozen shirts would come to fifteen dollars, which to a family in their circumstances would be a great help.

"Thank you, sir," said Paul. "My mother will accept the work thankfully, and will try to suit you. When shall I come for the cloth?"

46

"You may come to my house this evening, and I will give you a pattern, and an order for the materials on a dry goods dealer in Broadway."

"Where do you live, sir?"

"No. —— Madison Avenue, between Thirty-fourth and Thirty-fifth streets. My name is Preston. Can you remember it?"

"Yes, sir; but I will put it down to make sure."

"Well, good-morning."

"Good-morning, sir. I suppose you don't want a tie this morning?"

"I don't think you keep the kind I am accustomed to wear," said Mr. Preston, smiling. "I stick to the old fashions, and wear a stock."

A dry-goods store like the one where Mr. Preston got his start as a salesman.

The old gentleman had scarcely gone, when two boys of twelve or thirteen paused before the stand.

"That's a bully tie, Jeff!" said George, the elder of the two. "I have a good mind to buy it."

"It won't cost much," said Jeff. "Only twenty-five cents. But I like that one better."

"If you buy one, I will."

"All right," said Jeff, whose full name was Jefferson. "We can wear them to dancing-school this afternoon."

So the two boys bought a necktie, and this, in addition to previous sales, made six sold during the morning.

"I hope I shall do as well as I did yesterday," thought Paul. "If I can make nine shillings every day I won't complain. It is better than selling prize-packages."

Paul seemed likely to obtain his wish, since at twelve o'clock, when he returned home to dinner, he had sold ten ties, making rather more than half of the previous day's sales.

Mrs. Hoffman had been out once more, but met with no better success than before. There seemed to be no room anywhere for a new hand. At several places she had seen others, out of employment like herself, who were also in quest of work. The only encouragement she received was that probably in a month or six weeks business might so far improve that she could obtain work. But to Mrs. Hoffman it was a serious matter to remain idle even four weeks. She reflected that Paul's present employment was only temporary, and that he would be forced to give up his post as soon as George Barry should recover his health, which probably would be within a week or two. She tried in vain to think of some temporary employment, and determined, in case she should be unsuccessful in the afternoon, which she hardly anticipated, to consult Paul what she had better do.

Paul noticed when he came in that his mother looked more sober and thoughtful than usual.

"Have you a headache, mother?" he inquired.

"No, Paul," she said, smiling faintly.

"Something troubles you, I am sure," continued Paul.

"You are right, Paul," said Mrs. Hoffman, "though I didn't mean to tell you till evening."

"What is it?" asked Paul, anxiously.

48

"When I carried back the last shirts I made for Duncan & Co., they told me I couldn't have any more for a month or six weeks."

"That will give you some time to rest, mother," said Paul, who wanted to keep back his good news for a while.

"But I can't afford to rest, Paul."

"You forget that I am earning money, mother. I am sure I can earn a dollar a day."

"I know you are a good, industrious boy, Paul, and I don't know how we should get along without you. But it is necessary for me to do my part, though it is small."

"Don't be anxious, mother; I am sure we can get along."

"But I am not willing that the whole burden of supporting the family should come upon you. Besides, you are not sure how long you can retain your present employment."

"I know that, mother; but something else will be sure to turn up. If I can't do anything else, I can turn bootblack, though I would prefer something else. There is no chance of my being out of work long."

"There are fewer things for me to do," said his mother, "but perhaps you can think of something. I shall go out this afternoon, and try my luck once more. If I do not succeed, I will consult with you this evening."

"Suppose I tell you that I have work for you, enough to last for two or three weeks, that will pay five times as well as the work you have been doing; what would you say to that?" asked Paul, smiling.

"Are you in earnest, Paul?" asked his mother, very much surprised.

"Quite in earnest, mother. There's a gentleman up-town that wants a dozen shirts made, and is willing to pay ten shillings apiece."

"Ten shillings! Why, that's a dollar and a quarter."

"Of course it is. I told him I thought you would accommodate him."

"You are sure I can get the work to do?"

"Certainly. I am to go up to his house this evening and get the pattern and an order for the materials."

"It seems too good to be true," said his mother. "Why, I can earn at least a dollar a day."

"Then you will be doing as well as I am."

"Tell me how you heard of it, Paul," said Mrs. Hoffman.

Paul told the story of the manner in which he formed Mr. Preston's acquaintance.

"It's lucky you ran into him, Paul," said Jimmy.

"He didn't think so at the time," said Paul, laughing. "He said I nearly knocked the breath out of him."

"You won't go out this afternoon, mother, will you?" asked Jimmy.

"No, it will not be necessary now; I didn't think this morning that such a piece of good luck was in store for me."

CHAPTER X

ANOTHER LOSS

After supper Paul brushed his clothes carefully and prepared to go to the address given him by Mr. Preston. He decided to walk one way, not wishing to incur the expenses of two railroad fares.

The distance was considerable, and it was nearly eight o'clock when he arrived at his destination.

Paul found himself standing before a handsome house of brown stone. He ascended the steps, and inquired, on the door being opened, if Mr. Preston was at home.

"I'll see," said the servant.

She returned in a short time, and said: "He says you may come upstairs."

Paul followed the servant, who pointed out a door at the head of the first staircase.

Paul knocked, and, hearing "Come in" from within, he opened the door and entered.

He found himself in a spacious chamber, handsomely furnished. Mr. Preston, in dressing-gown and slippers, sat before a cheerful, open fire.

"Come and sit down by the fire," he said, sociably.

"Thank you, sir, I am warm with walking," and Paul took a seat near the door.

"I am one of the cold kind," said Mr. Preston, "and have a fire earlier than most people. You come about the shirts, I suppose?"

"Yes, sir."

"Will your mother undertake them?"

"With pleasure, sir. She can no longer get work from the shop."

"Business dull, I suppose?"

"Yes, sir."

"Then I am glad I thought of giving her the commission. How's business with you to-day, eh?"

"Pretty good, sir."

"How many neckties did you sell?"

"Nineteen, sir."

"And how much do you get for that?"

Nine shillings and a half—a dollar and eighteen cents."

51

"That's pretty good for a boy like you. When I was of your age I was working on a farm for my board and clothes."

"Were you, sir?" asked Paul, interested.

"Yes, I was bound out till I was twenty-one. At the end of that time I was to receive a hundred dollars and a freedom suit to begin the world with. That wasn't a very large capital, eh?"

"No, sir."

"But the death of my employer put an end to my apprenticeship at the age of eighteen. I hadn't a penny of money and was thrown upon my own resources. However, I had a pair of good strong arms, and a good stock of courage. I knew considerable about farming, but I didn't like it. I thought I should like trade better. So I went to the village merchant, who kept a small dry-goods store, and arranged with him to supply me with a small stock of goods, which I undertook to sell on commission for him.\ His business was limited, and having confidence in my honesty, he was quite willing to entrust me with what I wanted. So I set out with my pack on my back and made a tour of the neighboring villages."

Paul listened with eager interest. He had his own way to make, and it was very encouraging to find that Mr. Preston, who was evidently rich and prosperous, was no better off at eighteen than he was now.

"You will want to know how I succeeded. Well, at first only moderately; but I think I had some tact in adapting myself to the different classes of persons with whom I came in contact; at any rate, I was always polite, and that helped me. So my sales increased, and I did a good thing for my employer as well as myself. He would have been glad to employ me for a series of years, but I happened to meet a traveling salesman of a New York wholesale house, who offered to obtain me a position similar to his own. As this would give me a larger field and larger profits, I accepted gladly, and so changed the nature of my employment. I became very successful. My salary was raised from time to time, till it reached five thousand dollars. I lived frugally and saved money, and at length bought an interest in the house by which I had been so long employed. I am now senior partner, and, as you may suppose, very comfortably provided for.

"Do you know why I have told you this?" asked Mr. Preston, noticing the eagerness with which Paul had listened.

"I don't know, sir; but I have been very much interested."

"It is because I like to give encouragement to boys and young men who are now situated as I used to be. I think you are a smart boy."

"Thank you, sir."

"And, though you are poor, you can lift yourself to prosperity, if you are willing to work hard enough and long enough."

"I am not afraid of work," said Paul, promptly.

"No, I do not believe you are. I can tell by a boy's face, and you have the appearance of one who is willing to work hard. How long have you been a street peddler?"

"About a year, sir. Before that time my father was living, and I was kept at school."

"You will find the street a school, though of a different kind, in which you can learn valuable lessons. If you can get time in the evening, however, it will be best to keep up your school studies."

"I am doing that now, sir."

"That is well. And now, about the shirts. Did your mother say how long it would take her to make them?"

"About three weeks, I think, sir. Will that be soon enough?"

"That will do. Perhaps it will be well, however, to bring half the number whenever they are finished."

"All right, sir."

"I suppose your mother can cut them out if I send a shirt as a pattern?"

"Yes, sir."

Mr. Preston rose, and, going to a bureau, took therefrom a shirt which he handed to Paul. He then wrote a few lines on a slip of paper, which he also handed our hero.

"That is an order on Barclay & Co.," he explained, "for the requisite materials. If either you or your mother presents it, they will be given you."

"Very good, sir," said Paul.

He took his cap, and prepared to go.

"Good-evening, Mr. Preston," he said.

"Good-evening. I shall expect you with the shirts when they are ready."

Paul went downstairs and into the street, thinking that Mr. Preston was very sociable and agreeable. He had fancied that rich men were generally "stuck up," but about Mr. Preston there seemed an absence of all pretense. Paul's ambition was aroused when he thought of the story he had heard, and he wondered whether it would be possible for him to raise himself to wealth and live in as handsome a house as Mr. Preston. He thought what a satisfaction it would be if the time should ever come when he could free his mother from the necessity of work, and give little Jimmy a chance to develop his talent for drawing. However, such success must be a long way off, if it ever came.

He had intended to ride home, but his mind was so preoccupied that he forgot all about it, and had got some distance on his way before it occurred to him. Then, not feeling particularly tired, he concluded to keep on walking, as he had commenced.

"It will save me six cents," he reflected, "and that is something. If I am ever going to be a prosperous merchant, I must begin to save now."

So he kept on walking. Passing the Cooper Institute, he came into the Bowery, a broad and busy street, the humble neighbor of Broadway, to which it is nearly parallel.

He was still engaged in earnest thought, when he felt a rude slap on the back. Looking round, he met the malicious glance of Mike Donovan, who probably would not have ventured on such a liberty if he had not been accompanied by a boy a head taller than himself, and, to judge from appearances, of about the same character.

"What did you do that for, Mike?" demanded Paul.

"None of your business. I didn't hurt you, did I?" returned Mike, roughly.

"No, but I don't care to be hit that way by you."

"So you're putting on airs, are you?"

"No, I don't do that," returned Paul; "but I don't care about having anything to do with you."

"That's because you've got a new shirt, is it?" sneered Mike.

"It isn't mine."

"That's what I thought. Who did you steal it from?"

"Do you mean to insult me, Mike Donovan?" demanded Paul, angrily.

"Just as you like," said Mike, independently.

"If you want to know why I don't want to have anything to do with you, I will tell you."

"Tell ahead."

"Because you're a thief."

54

"If you say that again, I'll lick you," said Mike, reddening with anger.

"It's true. You stole my basket of candy the other day, and that isn't the only time you've been caught stealing."

"I'll give you the worst licking you ever had. Do you want to fight?" said Mike, flourishing his fist.

"No, I don't," said Paul. "Some time when I haven't a bundle, I'll accommodate you."

"You're a coward!" sneered Mike, gaining courage as he saw Paul was not disposed for an encounter.

"I don't think I am," said Paul, coolly.

"I'll hold your shirt," said Mike's companion, with a grin, "if you want to fight."

Paul, however, did not care to entrust the shirt to a stranger of so unprepossessing an appearance.

He, therefore, attempted to pass on. But Mike, encouraged by his reluctance, stepped up and shook his fist within an inch of Paul's nose, calling him at the same time a coward. This was too much for Paul's self-restraint. He dropped the shirt and pitched into Mike in so scientific a manner that the latter was compelled to retreat, and finally to flee at the top of his speed, not without having first received several pretty hard blows.

"I don't think he will meddle with me again," said Paul to himself, as he pulled down the sleeves of his jacket.

He walked back, and looked for the shirt which he had laid down before commencing the combat. But he looked in vain. Nothing was to be seen of the shirt or of Mike's companion. Probably both had disappeared together.

—

CHAPTER XI

BARCLAY & CO.

The loss of the shirt was very vexatious. It was not so much the value of it that Paul cared for, although this was a consideration by no means to be despised by one in his circumstances; but it had been lent as a pattern, and without it his mother would be unable to make Mr. Preston's shirts. As to recovering it, he felt that there was little chance of this. Besides, it would involve delay, and his mother could not afford to remain idle. Paul felt decidedly uncomfortable. Again Mike Donovan had done him an injury, and this time of a more serious nature than before.

What should he do?

There seemed but one answer to this question. He must go back to Mr. Preston, explain the manner in which he had lost his shirt, and ask him for another, promising, of course, to supply the place of the one lost. He was not sure whether Mr. Preston would accept this explanation. He might think it was only an attempt to defraud him. But, at any rate, it seemed the only thing to do, and it must be done at once. He entered a passing car, for it was too late to walk.

"I wish I had taken the car down," thought Paul. "Then I shouldn't have lost the shirt."

But it was too late for regrets now. He must do the best that remained to him.

It was nearly ten o'clock when Paul once more stood before the door of Mr. Preston's boarding-place. He rang the bell and asked to see him.

"You have been here before this evening?" said the servant.

"Yes."

"Then you know the room. You can walk right up."

Paul went upstairs and knocked at Mr. Preston's room. He was bidden to come in, and did so.

Mr. Preston looked up with surprise.

"I suppose you are surprised to see me," said Paul, rather awkwardly.

"Why, yes. I did not anticipate that pleasure quite so soon," said Mr. Preston, smiling.

"I am afraid it won't be a pleasure, for I bring bad news."

"Bad news?" repeated the gentleman, rather startled.

56

"Yes; I have lost the shirt you gave me."

"Oh, is that all?" said Mr. Preston, looking relieved. "But how did you lose it?"

"I was walking home down the Bowery, when two fellows met me. One of them, Mike Donovan, forced me into a fight. I gave him a licking," added Paul, with satisfaction; "but when it was all over, I found the other fellow had run off with the shirt."

"I don't believe it will fit him," said Mr. Preston, laughing.

As the speaker probably weighed two hundred and fifty pounds, it was, indeed, rather doubtful. Paul couldn't help laughing himself at the thought.

"You were certainly unlucky," said Mr. Preston. "Did you know the boy you fought with?"

"Yes, sir; he once before stole my stock of candy, when I was in the prize-package business."

"That was the day we got acquainted," remarked Mr. Preston.

"Yes, sir."

The Bowery neighborhood in New York. This is where the shirt is stolen from Paul.

"He doesn't seem to be a very particular friend of yours."

"No; he hates me, Mike does, though I don't know why. But I hope you won't be angry with me for losing the shirt?"

"No; it doesn't seem to be your fault, only your misfortune."

"I was afraid you might think I had made up the story, and only wanted to get an extra shirt from you."

"No, my young friend; I have some faith in physiognomy, and you have an honest face. I don't believe you would deceive me."

"No, I wouldn't," said Paul, promptly. "If you will trust me with another shirt, mother will make you an extra one to make up for the one I have lost."

"Certainly you shall have the extra shirt, but you needn't supply the place of the one lost."

"It is only fair that I should."

"That may be, and I am glad you made the offer, but the loss is of little importance to me. It was no fault of yours that you lost it, and you shall not suffer for it."

"You are very kind, sir," said Paul, gratefully.

"Only just, Paul."

Mr. Preston went to the bureau, and drew out another shirt, which he handed to Paul.

"Let me suggest, my young friend," he said, "that you ride home this time. It is late, and you might have another encounter with your friend. I should like to see him with the shirt on," and Mr. Preston laughed heartily at the thought.

Paul decided to follow his patron's advice. He had no idea of running any more risk in the matter. He accordingly walked to Fourth Avenue and got on board the car.

It was nearly eleven o'clock when he reached home. As it was never his habit to stay out late, his mother had become alarmed at his long absence.

"What kept you so late, Paul?" she asked.

"I'll tell you, pretty soon, mother. Here's the shirt that is to serve as a pattern. Can you cut out the new shirts by it?"

Mrs. Hoffman examined it attentively.

"Yes," she said; "there will be no difficulty about that. Mr. Preston must be a pretty large man."

"Yes, he is big enough for an alderman; but he is very kind and considerate, and I like him. You shall judge for yourself when I tell you what happened this evening."

It will not be necessary to tell Paul's adventure over again. His mother listened with pardonable indignation against Mike Donovan and his companion.

"I hope you won't have anything to do with that bad boy, Paul," she said.

"I shan't, if I can help it," said Paul. "I didn't want to speak to him to-night, but I couldn't help myself. Oh, I forgot to say, when half the shirts are ready, I am to take them to Mr. Preston."

"I think I can make one a day."

"There is no need of working so steadily, mother. You will be well paid, you know."

"That is true; and for that reason I shall work more cheerfully. I wish I could get paid as well for all my work."

"Perhaps Mr. Preston will recommend you to his friends, and you can get more work that way."

"I wish I could."

"I will mention it to him, when I carry back the last half dozen."

"Is he going to send the cloth?"

"I nearly forgot that, too. I have an order on Barclay & Co. for the necessary amount of cloth. I can go up there to-morrow morning and get it."

"That will take you from your work, Paul."

"Well, I can close up for a couple of hours."

"I don't think that will be necessary. I will go up myself and present the order, and get them to send it home for me."

"Will they do that?"

"It is their custom. Or, if the bundle isn't too large, I can bring it home myself in the car."

"That's all right, then. And now, mother, as it's past eleven o'clock, I think we may as well both go to bed."

The next day Paul went as usual to his business, and Mrs. Hoffman, after clearing away the breakfast, put on her bonnet and shawl, and prepared to go for the materials for the shirts.

The retail store of Barclay & Co. is of great size, and ranks among the most important in New York. It was not so well filled when Mrs. Hoffman entered as it would be later. She was directed to the proper counter, where she presented the order, signed by Mr. Preston. As he was a customer of long standing, there was no difficulty about filling the order. A bundle was made up, which, as it contained the materials for twelve shirts, necessarily was of considerable size.

"Here is your bundle, ma'am," said the clerk.

Mrs. Hoffman's strength was slender, and she did not feel able to carry the heavy bundle offered her. Even if she took the car, she would be obliged to carry it a portion of the way, and she felt that it would overtask her strength.

"Don't you send bundles?" she asked.

"Sometimes," said the clerk, looking superciliously at the modest attire of the poor widow, and mentally deciding that she was not entitled to much consideration. Had she been richly dressed, he would have been very obsequious, and insisted on sending home the smallest parcel. But there are many who have two rules of conduct, one for the rich, and quite a different one for the poor, and among these was the clerk who was attending upon Mrs. Hoffman.

"Then," said Mrs. Hoffman, "I should like to have you send this."

"It's a great deal of trouble to send everything," said the clerk, impertinently.

"This bundle is too heavy for me to carry," said the widow, deprecatingly.

"I suppose we can send it," said the clerk, ill-naturedly, "if you insist upon it."

Meanwhile, though he had not observed it, his employer had approached, and heard the last part of the colloquy. He was considered by some as a hard man, but there was one thing he always required of those in his employ; that was to treat all purchasers with uniform courtesy, whatever their circumstances.

"Are you objecting to sending this lady's bundle?" said Mr. Barclay, sternly.

The clerk looked up in confusion.

"I told her we would send it," he stammered.

"I have heard what passed. You have been deficient in politeness. If this happens again, you leave my employ."

"I will take your address," said the clerk, in a subdued tone.

Mrs. Hoffman gave it, and left the store, thankful for the interference of the great merchant who had given his clerk a lesson which the latter, as he valued his situation, found it advisable to bear in mind.

CHAPTER XII

THE BARREL THIEF

While Mike Donovan was engaged in his contest with Paul, his companion had quietly walked off with the shirt. It mattered very little to him which party conquered, as long as he carried off the spoils. His conduct in the premises was quite as unsatisfactory to Mike as it was to Paul. When Mike found himself in danger of being overpowered, he appealed to his companion for assistance, and was incensed to see him coolly disregarding the appeal, and selfishly appropriating the booty.

"The mane thafe!" he exclaimed after the fight was over, and he was compelled to retreat. "He let me be bate, and wouldn't lift his finger to help me. I'd like to put a head on him, I would."

Just at that moment Mike felt quite as angry with his friend, Jerry McGaverty, as with his late opponent.

"The shirt's mine, fair," he said to himself, "and I'll make Jerry give it to me."

But Jerry had disappeared, and Mike didn't know where to look for him. In fact, he had entered a dark alleyway, and, taking the shirt from the paper in which it was wrapped, proceeded to examine his prize.

The unusual size struck him.

"By the powers," he muttered, "it's big enough for me great-grandfather and all his children. I wouldn't like to pay for the cloth it tuck to make it. But I'll wear it, anyway."

Jerry was not particular as to an exact fit. His nether garments were several sizes too large for him, and the shirt would complete his costume appropriately. He certainly did need a new shirt, for the one he had on was the only article of the kind he possessed, and was so far gone that its best days, if it ever had any, appeared to date back to a remote antiquity. It had been bought cheap in Baxter street, its previous history being unknown.

Jerry decided to make the change at once. The alley afforded a convenient place for making the transfer. He accordingly pulled off the ragged shirt he wore and put on the article he had purloined from Paul. The sleeves were too long, but he turned up the cuffs, and the ample body he tucked inside his pants.

"It fits me too much," soliloquized Jerry, as he surveyed himself after the exchange. "I could let out the half of it, and have enough left for meself. Anyhow, it's clane, and it came chape enough."

He came out of the alley, leaving his old shirt behind him. Even if it had been worth carrying away, Jerry saw no use in possessing more than one shirt. It was his habit to wear one until it was ready to drop off from him, and then get another if he could. There is a practical convenience in this arrangement, though there are also objections which will readily occur to the reader.

On the whole, though the shirt fitted him too much, as he expressed it, he regarded himself complacently.

The superabundant material gave the impression of liberal expenditure and easy circumstances, since a large shirt naturally costs more than a small one. So Jerry, as he walked along the Bowery, assumed a jaunty air, precisely such as some of my readers may when they have a new suit to display. His new shirt was quite conspicuous, since he was encumbered neither with vest nor coat.

Mike, feeling sore over his defeat, met Jerry the next morning on Chatham street. His quick eye detected the improved state of his friend's apparel, and his indignation rose, as he reflected that Jerry had pocketed the profits while the hard knocks had been his.

"Jerry!" he called out.

Jerry did not see fit to heed the call. He was sensible that Mike had something to complain of, and he was in no hurry to meet his reproaches.

"Jerry McGaverty!" called Mike, coming near.

"Oh, it's you, Mike, is it?" answered Jerry, unable longer to keep up the pretense of not hearing.

"Yes, it's me," said Mike. "What made you leave me for last night?"

"I didn't want to interfere betwane two gintlemen," said Jerry, with a grin. "Did you mash him, Mike?"

"No," said Mike, sullenly, "he mashed me. Why didn't you help me?"

"I thought you was bating him, so, as I had some business to attind to, I went away."

"You went away wid the shirt."

"Yes, I took it by mistake. Ain't it an illigant fit?"

"It's big enough for two of you."

"Maybe I'll grow to it in time," said Jerry.

62

"And how much are you goin' to give me for my share?" demanded Mike.

"Say that ag'in," said Jerry.

Mike repeated it.

"I thought maybe I didn't hear straight. It ain't yours at all. Didn't I take it?"

"You wouldn't have got it if I hadn't fit with Paul."

"That ain't nothin' to me," said Jerry. "The shirt's mine, and I'll kape it."

Mike felt strongly tempted to "put a head on" Jerry, whatever that may mean; but, as Jerry was a head taller already, the attempt did not seem quite prudent. He indulged in some forcible remarks, which, however, did not disturb Jerry's equanimity.

"I'll give you my old shirt, Mike," he said, "if you can find it. I left it in an alley near the Old Bowery."

"I don't want the dirty rag," said Mike, contemptuously.

Finally a compromise was effected, Jerry offering to help Mike on the next occasion, and leave the spoils in his hands.

I have to chronicle another adventure of Jerry's, in which he was less fortunate than he had been in the present case. He was a genuine vagabond, and lived by his wits, being too lazy to devote himself to any regular street employment, as boot blacking or selling newspapers. Occasionally he did a little work at each of these, but regular, persistent industry was out of his line. He was a drone by inclination, and a decided enemy to work. On the subject of honesty his principles were far from strict. If he could appropriate what did not belong to him he was ready to do so without scruple. This propensity had several times brought him into trouble, and he had more than once been sent to reside temporarily on Blackwell's Island, from which he had returned by no means improved.

Mike was not quite so much of a vagabond as his companion. He could work at times, though he did not like it, and once pursued the vocation of a bootblack for several months with fair success.

But Jerry's companionship was doing him no good, and it seemed likely that eventually he would become quite as shiftless as Jerry himself.

Jerry, having no breakfast, strolled down to one of the city markets. He frequently found an opportunity of stealing here, and was now in search of such a chance. He was a dexterous and experienced barrel thief, a term which it may be necessary to explain. Barrels, then, have a commercial value, and coopers will generally pay twenty-five cents for one in good condition. This is enough, in the eyes of many a young vagabond, to pay for the risk incurred in stealing one.

Jerry prowled round the market for some time, seeking a good opportunity to walk off with an apple or banana, or something eatable. But the guardians of the stands seemed unusually vigilant, and he was compelled to give up the attempt, as involving too great risk. Jerry was hungry, and hunger is an uncomfortable feeling. He began to wish he had remained satisfied with his old shirt, dirty as it was, and carried the new one to some of the Baxter street dealers, from whom he could perhaps have got fifty cents for it. Now, fifty cents would have paid for a breakfast and a couple of cigars, and those just now would have made Jerry happy.

"What a fool I was not to think of it!" he said. "The old shirt would do me, and I could buy a bully breakfast wid the money I'd get for this."

Just at this moment he espied an empty barrel—a barrel apparently quite new and in an unguarded position. He resolved to take it, but the affair must be managed slyly.

He lounged up to the barrel, and leaned upon it indolently. Then, in apparent unconsciousness, he began to turn it, gradually changing its position. If observed, he could easily deny all felonious intentions. This he kept up till he got round the corner, when, glancing around to see if he was observed, he quickly lifted it on his shoulder and marched off.

All this happened without his being observed by the owner of the barrel. But a policeman, who chanced to be going his rounds, had been a witness of Jerry's little game. He remained quiet till Jerry's intentions became evident, then walked quietly up and put his hand on his shoulder.

"Put down that barrel!" he said, authoritatively.

Jerry had been indulging in visions of the breakfast he would get with the twenty-five cents he expected to obtain for the barrel, and the interruption was not an agreeable one. But he determined to brazen it out if possible.

"What for will I put it down?" he said.

"Because you have stolen it, that's why."

"No," said Jerry, "I'm carrying it round to my boss. It's his."

"Where do you work?"

"In Fourth Street," said Jerry, at random.

"What number?"

"No. 136."

"Then your boss will have to get someone in your place, for you will have to come with me."

"What for?"

"I saw you steal the barrel. You're a barrel thief, and this isn't the first time you've been caught at it. Carry back the barrel to the place you took it from and then come with me."

Jerry tried to beg off, but without avail.

At that moment Mike Donovan lounged up. When he saw his friend in custody, he felt a degree of satisfaction, remembering the trick Jerry had played on him.

"Where are you goin', Jerry?" he asked, with a grin, as he passed him. "Did ye buy that barrel to kape your shirt in?"

Jerry scowled but thought it best not to answer, lest his unlawful possession of the shirt might also be discovered, and lead to a longer sentence.

"He's goin' down to the island to show his new shirt," thought Mike, with a grin. "Maybe he'll set the fashion there."

Mike was right. Jerry was sent to the island for two months, there introducing Mr. Preston's shirt to company little dreamed of by its original proprietor.

CHAPTER XIII

OUT OF BUSINESS

The next day Mrs. Hoffman commenced work upon Mr. Preston's shirts. She worked with much more cheerfulness now that she was sure of obtaining a liberal price for her labor. As the shirts were of extra size, she found herself unable to finish one in a day, as she had formerly done, but had no difficulty in making four in a week. This, however, gave her five dollars weekly, instead of a dollar and a half as formerly. Now, five dollars may not seem a very large sum to some of my young readers, but to Mrs. Hoffman it seemed excellent compensation for a week's work.

"If I could only earn as much every week," she said to Paul on Saturday evening, "I should feel quite rich."

"Your work will last three weeks, mother, and perhaps at the end of that time some of Mr. Preston's friends may wish to employ you."

"I hope they will."

"How much do you think I have made?" continued Paul.

"Six dollars."

"Seven dollars and a half."

"So between us we have earned over twelve dollars."

"I wish I could earn something," said little Jimmy, looking up from his drawing.

"There's time enough for that, Jimmy. You are going to be a great artist one of these days."

"Do you really think I shall?" asked the little boy, wistfully.

"I think there is a good chance of it. Let me see what you are drawing."

The picture upon which Jimmy was at work represented a farmer standing upright in a cart, drawn by a sturdy, large-framed horse. The copy bore a close resemblance to the original, even in the most difficult portions—the face and expression, both in the man and the horse, being carefully reproduced.

"This is wonderful, Jimmy," exclaimed Paul, in real surprise. "Didn't you find it hard to get the man's face just right?"

"Rather hard," said Jimmy; "I had to be careful, but I like best the parts where I have to take the most pains."

"I wish I could afford to hire a teacher for you," said Paul. "Perhaps, if mother and I keep on earning so much money, we shall be able to some time."

By the middle of the next week six of the shirts were finished, and Paul, as had been agreed upon, carried them up to Mr. Preston. He was fortunate enough to find him at home.

"I hope they will suit you," said Paul.

"I can see that the sewing is excellent," said Mr. Preston, examining them. "As to the fit, I can tell better after I have tried one on."

"Mother made them just like the one you sent; but if there is anything wrong, she will, of course, be ready to alter them."

"If they are just like the pattern, they will be sure to suit me."

"And now, my young friend," he added, "let me know how you are getting on in your own business."

"I am making a dollar a day, sometimes a little more."

"That is very good."

"Yes, sir; but it won't last long."

"I believe you told me that the stand belonged to some one else."

"Yes, sir; I am only tending it in his sickness; but he is getting better, and when he gets about again, I shall be thrown out of business."

"But you don't look like one who would remain idle long."

"No, sir; I shall be certain to find something to do, if it is only blacking boots."

"Have you ever been in that business?"

"I've tried about everything," said Paul, laughing.

"I suppose you wouldn't enjoy boot-blacking much?"

"No, sir; but I would rather do that than be earning nothing."

"You are quite right there, and I am glad you have no false shame in the matter. There are plenty who have. For instance, a stout, broad-shouldered young fellow applied to me thus morning for a clerkship. He said he had come to the city in search of employment, and had nearly expended all his money without finding anything to do. I told him I couldn't give him a clerkship, but was in want of a porter. I offered him the place at two dollars per day. He drew back, and said he should not be willing to accept a porter's place."

"He was very foolish," said Paul.

"So I thought. I told him that if such were his feelings, I could not help him. Perhaps he may regret his refusal, when he is reduced to his last penny. By the way, whenever you have to give up your stand, you may come to me, and I will see what I can do for you."

"Thank you, sir."

"And now, about these shirts; I believe I agreed to pay a dollar and a quarter each."

"Yes, sir."

"As they are of extra size, I think I ought to pay twelve shillings, instead of ten."

"My mother thinks herself well paid at ten shillings."

"There must be a great deal of work about one. Twelve shillings are none too much," and Mr. Preston placed nine dollars in Paul's hand.

"Thank you," said Paul, gratefully. "My mother will consider herself very lucky."

When Mrs. Hoffman received from Paul a dollar and a half more than she anticipated, she felt in unusually good spirits. She had regretted the loss of her former poorly paid work, but it appeared that her seeming misfortune had only prepared the way for greater prosperity. The trouble was that it would not last. Still, it would tide over the dull time, and when this job was over, she might be able to resume her old employment. At any rate, while the future seemed uncertain, she did not feel like increasing her expenditures on account of her increased earnings, but laid carefully away three-quarters of her receipts to use hereafter in case of need.

Meanwhile, Paul continued to take care of George Barry's business. He had been obliged to renew the stock, his large sales having materially reduced it. Twice a week he went up to see his principal to report sales. George Barry could not conceal the surprise he felt at Paul's success.

"I never thought you would do so well," he said. "You beat me."

"I suppose it's because I like it," said Paul. "Then, as I get only half the profits, I have to work the harder to make fair wages."

"It is fortunate for my son that he found you to take his place," said Mrs. Barry. "He could not afford to lose all the income from his business."

"It is a good thing for both of us," said Paul. "I was looking for a job just when he fell sick."

"What had you been doing before?"

"I was in the prize-package business, but that got played out, and I was a gentleman at large, seeking for a light, genteel business that wouldn't require much capital."

"I shall be able to take my place pretty soon now," said the young man. "I might go to-morrow, but mother thinks it imprudent."

"Better get back your strength first, George," said his mother, "or you may fall sick again."

But her son was impatient of confinement and anxious to get to work again. So, two days afterward, about the middle of the forenoon, Paul was surprised by seeing George Barry get out of a Broadway omnibus, just in front of the stand.

"Can I sell you a necktie, Mr. Barry?" he asked, in a joke.

"I almost feel like a stranger," said Barry, "it's so long since I have been here."

"Do you feel strong enough to take charge now?" asked Paul.

"I am not so strong as I was, and the walk from our rooms would tire me; but I think if I rode both ways for the present I shall be able to get along."

"Then you won't need me any longer?"

"I would like to have you stay with me to-day. I don't know how I shall hold out."

"All right! I'll stop."

George Barry remained in attendance the rest of the day. He found that his strength had so far returned that he should be able to manage alone hereafter, and he told Paul so.

"I am glad you are well again, George," said Paul. "It must have been dull work staying at home sick."

"Yes, it was dull; but I felt more comfortable from knowing that you were taking my place. If I get sick again I will send for you."

"I hope you won't get sick; but if you do, I will do what I can to help you."

So the two parted on the best of terms. Each had been of service to the other, and neither had cause to complain.

"Well," said Paul to himself, "I am out of work again. What shall I go at next?"

It was six o'clock, and there was nothing to be done till the morrow. He went slowly homeward, revolving this subject in his mind. He knew that he need not remain idle. He could black boots, or sell newspapers, if nothing better offered, and he thought it quite possible that he might adopt the latter business, for a few days at least. He had not forgotten Mr. Preston's injunction to let him know when he got out of business; but, as the second half dozen shirts would be ready in three or four days, he preferred to wait till then, and not make a special call on Mr. Preston. He had considerable independence of feeling, and didn't like to put himself in the position of one asking a favor, though he had no objection to accept one voluntarily offered.

"Well, mother," he said, entering his humble home, "I am out of business."

"Has George recovered, then?"

"Yes, he was at the stand to-day, but wanted me to stay with him till this evening."

"Oh, I'm so sorry!" said Jimmy.

"Sorry that George has got well? For shame, Jimmy!"

"No, I don't mean that, Paul. I am sorry you are out of work."

"I shall find plenty to do, Jimmy. Perhaps Mr. Stewart will take me in as senior partner, if I ask him."

"I don't think he will," said Jimmy, laughing.

"Then perhaps I can get a few scholars in drawing. Can't you recommend me?"

"I am afraid not, Paul, unless you have improved a good deal."

CHAPTER XIV

THE DIAMOND RING

Paul was up betimes the next morning. He had made up his mind for a few days, at least, to sell newspapers, and it was necessary in this business to begin the day early. He tool a dollar with him and invested a part of it in a stock of dailies. He posted himself in Printing House square, and began to look out for customers. Being an enterprising boy, he was sure to meet with fair success in any business which he undertook. So it happened that at ten o'clock he had sold out his stock of papers, and realized a profit of fifty cents.

It was getting late for morning papers, and there was nothing left to do till the issue of the first edition of the afternoon papers.

"I'll go down and see how George Barry is getting along," thought Paul.

He crossed Broadway and soon reached the familiar stand.

"How's business, George?" he inquired.

"Fair," said Barry. "I've sold four ties."

"How do you feel?"

"I'm not so strong as I was, yet. I get tired more easily. I don't think I shall stay in this business long."

"You don't? What will you do then?"

"I've got a chance in Philadelphia, or I shall have by the first of the month."

"What sort of a chance?"

"Mother got a letter yesterday from a cousin of hers who has a store on Chestnut street. He offers to take me as a clerk, and give me ten dollars a week at first, and more after a while."

"That's a good offer. I should like to get one like it."

"I'll tell you what, Paul, you'd better buy out my stand. You know how to sell ties, and can make money."

"There's only one objection, George."

"What's that?"

"I haven't got any capital."

"It don't need much."

"How much?"

"I'll sell out all my stock at cost price."

"How much do you think there is?"

71

"About twenty-five dollars' worth. Then there is the frame, which is worth, say ten dollars, making thirty-five in all. That isn't much."

"It's more than I've got. I'll tell you what I'll do. I'll take it, and pay you five dollars down and the rest in one month."

"I would take your offer, Paul, but I need all the money how. It will be expensive moving to Philadelphia and I shall want all I can get."

"I wish I could buy you out," said Paul, thoughtfully.

"Can't you borrow the money?"

"How soon do you want to give up?"

"It's the seventeenth now. I should like to get rid of it by the twenty-second."

"I'll see what I can do. Just keep it for me till to-morrow."

"All right."

Paul walked home revolving in his mind this unexpected opportunity. He had made, as George Barry's agent, a dollar a day, though he received only half the profits. If he were himself the proprietor, and did equally well, he could make twelve dollars a week. The calculation almost took away his breath. Twelve dollars a week would make about fifty dollars a month. It would enable him to contribute more to the support of the family, and save up money besides. But the great problem was, how to raise the necessary money. If Paul had been a railroad corporation, he might have issued first mortgage bonds at a high rate of interest, payable in gold, and negotiated them through some leading banker. But he was not much versed in financial schemes, and therefore was at a loss. The only wealthy friend he had was Mr. Preston, and he did not like to apply to him till he had exhausted other ways and means.

"What makes you so sober, Paul?" asked his mother, as he entered the room. "You are home early."

"Yes, I sold all my papers, and thought I would take an early dinner, so as to be on hand in time for the first afternoon papers."

"Don't you feel well?"

"Tiptop; but I've had a good offer, and I'm thinking whether I can accept it."

"What sort of an offer?"

"George Barry wants to sell out his stand."

"How much does he ask?"

"Thirty-five dollars."

"Is it worth that?"

"Yes, it's worth all that, and more, too. If I had it I could make two dollars a day. But I haven't got thirty-five dollars."

"I can let you have nine, Paul. I had a little saved up, and I haven't touched the money Mr. Preston paid me for the shirts."

"I've got five myself, but that will only make fourteen."

"Won't he wait for the rest?"

"No, he's going to Philadelphia early next week, and wants the whole in cash."

"It would be a pity to lose such a good chance," said Mrs. Hoffman.

"That's what I think."

"You could soon save up the money on two dollars a day."

"I could pay for it in a month—I mean, all above the fourteen dollars we have."

"In a day or two I shall have finished the second half-dozen shirts, and then I suppose Mr. Preston will pay me nine dollars more. I could let you have six dollars of that."

"That would make twenty. Perhaps George Barry will take that. If he won't I don't know but I will venture to apply to Mr. Preston."

"He seems to take an interest in you. Perhaps he would trust you with the money."

"I could offer him a mortgage on the stock," said Paul.

"If he has occasion to foreclose, he will be well provided with neckties," said Mrs. Hoffman, smiling.

"None of which he could wear. I'll tell you what, mother, I should like to pick up a pocketbook in the street, containing, say, twenty or twenty-five dollars."

"That would be very convenient," said his mother; "but I think it will hardly do to depend on such good luck happening to you. By the way," she said, suddenly, "perhaps I can help you, after all. Don't you remember that gold ring I picked up in Central Park two years ago?"

"The one you advertised?"

"Yes. I advertised, or, rather, your father did; but we never found an owner for it."

"I remember it now, mother. Have you got the ring still?"

I will get it."

Mrs. Hoffman went to her trunk, and, opening it, produced the ring referred to. It was a gold ring with a single stone of considerable size.

"I don't know how much it is worth," said Mrs. Hoffman; "but if the ring is a diamond, as I think it is, it must be worth as much as twenty dollars."

"Did you ever price it?"

"No, Paul; I have kept it, thinking that it would be something to fall back upon if we should ever be hard pressed. As long as we were able to get along without suffering, I thought I would keep it. Besides, I had another feeling. It might belong to some person who prized it very much, and the time might come when we could find the owner. However, that is not likely after so long a time. So, if you cannot raise the money in any other way, you may sell the ring."

"I might pawn it for thirty days, mother. By that time I should be able to redeem it with the profits of my business."

"I don't think you could get enough from a pawn-broker."

"I can try, at any rate; but first I will see George Barry, and find out whether he will take twenty dollars down, and the rest at the end of a month."

Paul wrapped up the ring in a piece of paper, and deposited it in his vest pocket. He waited till after dinner, and then went at once to the necktie stand, where he made the proposal to George Barry.

The young man shook his head.

"I'd like to oblige you, Paul," he said, "but I must have the money. I have an offer of thirty-two dollars, cash, from another party, and I must take up with it if I can't do any better. I'd rather sell out to you, but you know I have to consult my own interest."

"Of course, George, I can't complain of that."

"I think you will be able to borrow the money somewhere."

"Most of my friends are as poor as myself," said Paul. "Still, I think I shall be able to raise the money. Only wait for me two days."

"Yes, Paul, I'll wait that long. I'd like to sell out to you, if only because you have helped me when I was sick. But for you all that would have been lost time."

"Where there's a will there's a way, George," said Paul. "I'm bound to buy your stand and I will raise the money somehow."

Paul bought a few papers, for he did not like to lose the afternoon trade, and in an hour had sold them all off, realizing a profit of twenty cents. This made his profits for the day seventy cents.

"That isn't as well as I used to do," said Paul to himself, "but perhaps I can make something more by and by. I will go now and see what I can get for the ring."

As he had determined, he proceeded to a pawnbroker's shop which he had often passed. It was on Chatham Street, and was kept by an old man, an Englishman by birth, who, though he lived meanly in a room behind his shop, was popularly supposed to have accumulated a considerable fortune.

CHAPTER XV

THE PAWNBROKER'S SHOP

Stuffed behind the counter, and on the shelves of the pawnbroker's shop, were articles in almost endless variety. All was fish that came to his net. He was willing to advance on anything that had a marketable value, and which promised to yield him, I was about to say, a fair profit. But a fair profit was far from satisfying the old man. He demanded an extortionate profit from those whom ill-fortune drove to his door for relief.

Eliakim Henderson, for that was his name, was a small man, with a bald head, scattering yellow whiskers, and foxlike eyes. Spiderlike he waited for the flies who flew of their own accord into his clutches, and took care not to let them go until he had levied a large tribute. When Paul entered the shop, there were three customers ahead of him. One was a young woman, whose pale face and sunken cheeks showed that she was waging an unequal conflict with disease. She was a seamstress by occupation, and had to work fifteen hours a day to earn the little that was barely sufficient to keep body and soul together. Confined in her close little room on the fourth floor, she scarcely dared to snatch time to look out of the window into the street beneath, lest she should not be able to complete her allotted task. A two days' sickness had compelled her to have recourse to Eliakim Henderson. She had under her arm a small bundle covered with an old copy of the Sun.

"What have you got there?" asked the old man, roughly. "Show it quick, for there's others waiting."

Meekly she unfolded a small shawl, somewhat faded from long use.

"What will you give me on that?" she asked, timidly.

"It isn't worth much."

"It cost five dollars."

"Then you got cheated. It never was worth half the money. What do you want on it?"

The seamstress intended to ask a dollar and a half, but after this depreciation she did not venture to name so high a figure.

"A dollar and a quarter," she said.

"A dollar and a quarter!" repeated the old man, shrilly. "Take it home with you. I don't want it."

"What will you give?" asked the poor girl, faintly.

"Fifty cents. Not a penny more."

"Fifty cents!" she repeated, in dismay, and was about to refold it. But the thought of her rent in arrears changed her half-formed intention.

"I'll take it, sir."

The money and ticket were handed her, and she went back to her miserable attic-room, coughing as she went.

"Now, ma'am," said Eliakim.

His new customer was an Irish woman, by no means consumptive in appearance, red of face and portly of figure.

"And what'll ye be givin' me for this?" she asked, displaying a pair of pantaloons.

"Are they yours, ma'am?" asked Eliakim, with a chuckle.

"It's not Bridget McCarty that wears the breeches," said that lady. "It's me husband's, and a dacent, respectable man he is, barrin' the drink, which turns his head. What'll ye give for 'em?"

"Name your price," said Eliakim, whose principle it was to insist upon his customers making the first offer.

"Twelve shillin's," said Bridget.

"Twelve shillings!" exclaimed Eliakim, holding up both hands. "That's all they cost when they were new."

"They cost every cint of five dollars," said Bridget. "They was made at one of the most fashionable shops in the city. Oh, they was an illigant pair when they was new."

"How many years ago was that?" asked the pawnbroker.

"Only six months, and they ain't been worn more'n a month."

"I'll give you fifty cents."

"Fifty cints!" repeated Mrs. McCarty, turning to the other customers, as if to call their attention to an offer so out of proportion to the valuable article she held in her hand. "Only fifty cints for these illigant breeches! Oh, it's you that's a hard man, that lives on the poor and the nady."

"You needn't take it. I should lose money on it, if you didn't redeem it."

"He says he'd lose money on it," said Mrs. McCarty. "And suppose he did, isn't he a-rollin' in gold?"

"I'm poor," said Eliakim; "almost as poor as you, because I'm too liberal to my customers."

—

77

"Hear till him!" said Mrs. McCarty. "He says he's liberal and only offers fifty cints for these illigant breeches."

"Will you take them or leave them?" demanded the pawnbroker, impatiently.

"You may give me the money," said Bridget; "and it's I that wonder how you can slape in your bed, when you are so hard on poor folks."

Mrs. McCarty departed with her money, and Eliakim fixed his sharp eyes on the next customer. It was a tall man, shabbily dressed, with a thin, melancholy-looking face, and the expression of one who had struggled with the world, and failed in the struggle.

"How much for this?" he asked, pointing to the violin, and speaking in a slow, deliberate tone, as if he did not feel at home in the language.

"What do you want for it?"

"Ten dollar," he answered.

"Ten dollars! You're crazy!" was the contemptuous comment of the pawnbroker.

"He is a very good violin," said the man. "If you would like to hear him," and he made a movement as if to play upon it.

"Never mind!" said Eliakim. "I haven't any time to hear it. If it were new it would be worth something; but it's old, and——"

"But you do not understand," interrupted the customer, eagerly. "It is worth much more than new. Do you see, it is by a famous maker? I would not sell him, but I am poor, and my Bettina needs bread. It hurts me very much to let him go. I will buy him back as soon as I can."

"I will give you two dollars, but I shall lose on it, unless you redeem it."

"Two dollar!" repeated the Italian. "Ocielo! it is nothing. But Bettina is at home without bread, poor little one! Will you not give three dollar?"

"Not a cent more."

"I will take it."

"There's your money and ticket."

And with these the poor Italian departed, giving one last lingering glance at his precious violin, as Eliakim took it roughly and deposited it upon a shelf behind him. But he thought of his little daughter at home, and the means of relief which he held in his hand,

and a smile of joy lightened his melancholy features. The future might be dark and unpromising, but for three days, at any rate, she should not want bread.

Paul's turn came next.

"What have you got?" asked the pawnbroker.

Paul showed the ring.

Eliakim took it, and his small, beadlike eyes sparkled avariciously as he recognized the diamond, for his experience was such that he could form a tolerably correct estimate of its value. But he quickly suppressed all outward manifestations of interest, and said, indifferently, "What do you want for it?"

"I want twenty dollars," said Paul, boldly.

"Twenty dollars!" returned the pawnbroker. "That's a joke."

"No, it isn't," said Paul. "I want twenty dollars, and you can't have the ring for less."

"If you said twenty shillings, I might give it to you," said Eliakim; "but you must think I am a fool to give twenty dollars."

"That's cheap for a diamond ring," said Paul. "It's worth a good deal more."

The pawnbroker eyed Paul sharply. Did the boy know that it was a diamond ring? What chance was there of deceiving him as to its value? The old man, whose business made him a good judge, decided that the ring was not worth less than two hundred and fifty dollars, and if he could get it into his possession for a trifle, it would be a paying operation.

"You're mistaken, boy," he said. "It's not a diamond."

"What is it?"

"A very good imitation."

"How much is it worth?"

"I'll give you three dollars."

"That won't do. I want to raise twenty dollars, and if I can't get that, I'll keep the ring."

The pawnbroker saw that he had made a mistake. Paul was not as much in need of money as the majority of his customers. He would rather pay twenty dollars than lose the bargain, though it went against the grain to pay so much money. But after pronouncing the stone an imitation, how could he rise much above the offer he had already made? He resolved to approach it gradually. Surveying it more closely, he said:

"It is an excellent imitation. I will give you five dollars."

Paul was not without natural shrewdness, and this sudden advance convinced him that it was, after all, a real stone. He determined to get twenty dollars or carry the ring home.

"Five dollars won't do me any good," he said. "Give me back the ring."

"Five dollars is a good deal of money," said Eliakim.

"I'd rather have the ring."

"What is your lowest price?"

"Twenty dollars."

"I'll give you eight."

"Just now you said it was worth only three," said Paul, sharply.

"It is very fine gold. It is better than I thought. Here is the money."

"You're a little too fast," said Paul, coolly. "I haven't agreed to part with the ring for eight dollars, and I don't mean to. Twenty dollars is my lowest price."

"I'll give you ten," said the old man, whose eagerness increased with Paul's indifference.

"No, you won't. Give me back the ring."

"I might give eleven, but I should lose money."

"I don't want you to lose money, and I've concluded to keep the ring," said Paul, rightly inferring from the old man's eagerness that the ring was much more valuable than he had at first supposed.

But the old pawnbroker was fascinated by the sparkling bauble. He could not make up his mind to give it up. By fair means or foul he must possess it. He advanced his bid to twelve, fourteen, fifteen dollars, but Paul shook his head resolutely. He had made up his mind to carry it to Ball & Black's, or some other first-class jewelers, and ascertain whether it was a real diamond or not, and if so to obtain an estimate of its value.

"I've changed my mind," he said. "I'll keep the ring. Just give it back to me."

CHAPTER XVI

THE JEWELER'S PRICE

But to give it back was not Eliakim's intention. Should he buy it at twenty dollars, he would make at least two hundred, and such bargains were not to be had every day. He decided to give Paul his price.

"I will give you twenty dollars," he said; "but it is more than the ring is worth."

"I have concluded not to take twenty dollars," said Paul. "You may give it back."

"You agreed to take twenty dollars," said Eliakim, angrily.

"That was when I first came in. You said you wouldn't give it."

"I have changed my mind."

So have I," said Paul. "You had a chance to get it, but now it's too late."

Eliakim was deeply disappointed. Generally he had his own way with his customers, who, being in urgent need of money, were obliged to accept such terms as he chose to offer. But now the tables were turned, and Paul proved more than a match for him. He resolved to attempt intimidation.

"Boy, where did you get this ring?" he asked, in a significant tone.

"Honestly," said Paul. "That's all you need to know."

"I don't believe it," said the old man, harshly. "I believe you stole it."

"You may believe what you like, but you must give it back to me," said Paul, coolly.

"I've a great mind to call a policeman," said Eliakim.

"If you did," said Paul, "I'd tell him that you were anxious to get the ring, though you believed it to be stolen. Perhaps he might have something to say to you."

Eliakim perceived the force of Paul's argument, for in law the receiver of stolen goods is as bad as the thief, and there had been occasions when the pawnbroker had narrowly escaped punishment for thus indirectly conniving at theft.

"If you say you got it honestly, I'll buy it of you," he said, changing his tune. "What will you take?"

"I don't care about selling to-day," answered Paul.

"I'll give you twenty-five dollars."

"I can't sell without consulting my mother. It belongs to her."

Reluctantly Eliakim gave back the ring, finding his wiles of no effect.

"Bring your mother round to-morrow," he said. "I'll give you a better price than you will get anywhere else."

"All right," said Paul. "I'll tell her what you say."

The old pawnbroker followed Paul with wistful glances, vainly wishing that he had not at first depreciated the ring to such an extent, that his subsequent advances had evidently excited his customer's suspicion that it was more valuable than he supposed. He felt that he had lost it through not understanding the character of the boy with whom he had to deal.

"Well, Paul, what news of the ring?" asked Mrs. Hoffman, as he re-entered the room.

"I was offered twenty-five dollars for it," said Paul.

"Did you sell it?"

"No, mother."

"Why not?" asked Jimmy. "Twenty-five dollars is a lot of money."

"I know it," said Paul; "but the ring is worth a great deal more."

"What makes you think so, Paul?"

"Because the offer was made by a pawnbroker, who never pays quarter what an article is worth. I am sure the ring is worth a hundred dollars."

"Yes, I am sure it is worth all that."

"A hundred dollars!" repeated Jimmy, awestruck at the magnitude of the sum.

"What shall we do about it, Paul?" asked his mother. "A hundred dollars will do us more good than the ring."

"I know that, mother. What I propose is, to carry it to Ball & Black's, or Tiffany's, and sell it for whatever they say it is worth. They are first-class houses, and we can depend upon fair treatment."

"Your advice is good, Paul. I think we will follow it. When will you go?"

"I will go at once. I have nothing else to do, and I would like to find out as soon as I can how much it will bring. Old Henderson wanted me to think, at first, that it was only imitation, and offered me twenty shillings on it. He's an old cheat. When he found that I wasn't to be humbugged, he raised his offer by degrees to twenty-five dollars. That was what made me suspect its value."

"If you get a hundred dollars, Paul," said Jimmy, "you can buy out the stand."

"That depends on whether mother will lend me the money," said Paul. "You know it's hers. She may not be willing to lend without security."

"I am so unaccustomed to being a capitalist," said Mrs. Hoffman, smiling, "that I shan't know how to sustain the character. I don't think I shall be afraid to trust you, Paul."

Once more, with the ring carefully wrapped in a paper and deposited in his pocketbook, Paul started uptown. Tiffany, whose fame as a jeweler is world-wide, was located on Broadway. He had not yet removed to his present magnificent store on Union Square.

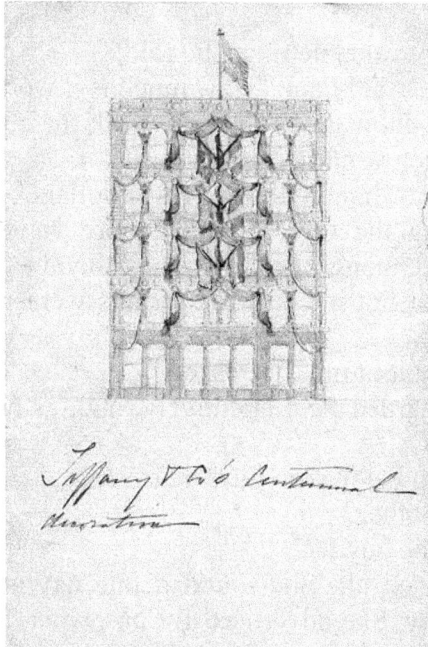

A watercolor of the Tiffany and Company headquarters building.

Paul knew the store, but had never entered it. Now, as he entered, he was struck with astonishment at the sight of the immense and costly stock, unrivaled by any similar establishment, not only in the United States, but in Europe. Our hero walked up to the counter, and stood beside a richly-dressed lady who was bargaining for a costly bracelet. He had to wait ten minutes while the lady was making her choice from a number submitted to her for inspection. Finally she selected one, and paid for it. The clerk, now being at leisure, turned to our hero and asked:—

"Well, young man, what can I do for you?"

"I have a ring which I should like to show you. I want to know how much it is worth."

"Very well. Let me see it."

When Paul produced the diamond ring, the clerk, who had long been in the business, and perceived its value at once, started in surprise.

"This is a very valuable ring," he said.

"So I thought," said Paul. "How much is it worth?"

"Do you mean how much should we ask for it?"

"No; how much would you give for it?"

"Probably two hundred and fifty dollars." Paul was quite startled on finding the ring so much more valuable than he had supposed. He had thought it might possibly be worth a hundred dollars; but he had not imagined any rings were worth as much as the sum named.

"Will you buy it of me?" he asked.

The clerk regarded Paul attentively, and, as he thought, a little suspiciously.

"Does the ring belong to you?" he asked.

"No, to my mother."

"Where did she buy it?"

"She didn't buy it at all. She found it one day at Central Park. It belongs to her now. She advertised for an owner, and examined the papers to see if it was advertised as lost, but could hear nothing of the one to whom it belonged."

"How long ago was this?"

"Two years ago."

"I will show this ring to Mr. Tiffany," said the clerk.

"Very well."

Paul took a seat and waited.

———

84

Soon Mr. Tiffany came up.

"Are you the boy who brought in the ring?" he asked.

"Yes, sir."

"You say your mother found it two years ago in Central Park?"

"Yes, sir."

"It is a valuable ring. I should be willing to buy it for two hundred and fifty dollars, if I were quite certain that you had a right to dispose of it."

"I have told you the truth, Mr. Tiffany," said Paul, a little nettled at having his word doubted.

"That may be, but there is still a possibility that the original owner may turn up."

"Won't you buy it, then?" asked Paul, disappointed, for, if he were unable to dispose of the ring, he would have to look elsewhere for the means of buying out Barry's street stand.

"I don't say that; but I should want a guaranty of indemnity against loss, in case the person who lost it should present a claim."

"In that case," said Paul, "I would give you back the money you paid me."

Mr. Tiffany smiled.

"But suppose the money were all spent," he suggested. "I suppose you are intending to use the money?"

"I am going to start in business with it," said Paul, "and I hope to add to it."

"Every one thinks so who goes into business; but some get disappointed. You see, my young friend, that I should incur a risk. Remember, I don't know you. I judge from your appearance that you are honest; but appearances are sometimes deceitful."

"Then I suppose you won't buy it?" said Paul, who saw the force of this remark.

"If you can bring here any responsible gentleman who knows you, and is willing to guarantee me against loss in the event of the owner's being found I will buy the ring for two hundred and fifty dollars."

Paul brightened up. He thought at once of Mr. Preston, and, from the friendly interest which that gentleman appeared to take in him, he judged that he would not refuse him this service.

"I think I can do that," he said. "Do you know Mr. Andrew Preston? He is a wealthy gentleman, who lives on Madison Avenue, between Thirty-fourth and Thirty-fifth streets."

"Not personally. I know him by reputation."

"Will he be satisfactory?"

"Entirely so."

"He knows me well," said Paul. "I think he will be willing to stand security for me. I will come back in a day or two."

A brown stone house on Madison Ave in New York.
Much like the house where Mr. Preston lives.

Paul took the ring, and left the store. He determined to call that evening on Mr. Preston, and ask the favor indicated.

CHAPTER XVII

MR. FELIX MONTGOMERY

Paul had an errand farther uptown, and, on leaving Tiffany's walked up as far as Twenty-third Street. Feeling rather tired, he got on board a University place car to return. They had accomplished, perhaps, half the distance, when, to his surprise, George Barry entered the car.

"How do you happen to be here, at this time, Barry?" he asked. "I thought you were attending to business."

"I closed up for a couple of hours, having an errand at home. Where have you been?"

"To Tiffany's."

"What, the jewelers?"

"Yes."

"To buy a diamond ring, I suppose," said Barry, jocosely.

"No—not to buy, but to sell one."

"You are joking," said his companion, incredulously.

"No, I am not. The ring belongs to my mother. I am trying to raise money enough on it to buy you out."

"I didn't know your mother was rich enough to indulge in such expensive jewelry."

"She isn't, and that's the reason I am trying to sell it."

"I mean, I didn't think she was ever rich enough."

"I'll explain it," said Paul. "The ring was found some time since in Central Park. As no owner has ever appeared, though we advertised it, we consider that it belongs to us."

"How much is it worth?"

"Mr. Tiffany offered two hundred and fifty dollars for it."

Barry uttered an exclamation of surprise.

"Well, that is what I call luck. Of course, you accepted it."

"I intend to do so; but I must bring some gentleman who will guarantee that I am all right and have the right to sell it."

"Can you do that?"

"I think so! I am going to ask Mr. Preston. I think he will do me that favor."

"Then there's a fair chance of your buying me out."

"Yes. I guess I can settle the whole thing up to-morrow."

"Have you got the ring with you?"

"Yes."

"I should like to see it, if you have no objection."

Paul drew it from his pocket, and passed it over to Barry.

"It's a handsome one, but who would think such a little thing could be worth two hundred and fifty dollars?"

"I'd rather have the money than the ring."

"So would I."

On the right of Paul sat a man of about forty, well-dressed and respectable in appearance, with a heavy gold chain ostentatiously depending from his watch pocket, and with the air of a substantial citizen. He listened to the conversation between Barry and Paul with evident interest, and when Barry had returned the ring, he said:

"Young gentleman, would you be kind enough to let me look at your ring? I am myself in business as a jeweler in Syracuse, and so feel an interest in examining it."

"Certainly, sir," said Paul, the stranger's explanation of his motives inspiring him with perfect confidence.

The jeweler from Syracuse took the ring in his hands and appeared to examine it carefully.

"This is a handsome ring," he said, "and one of great value. How much were you offered for it at Tiffany's?"

"Two hundred and fifty dollars."

"It is worth more."

"Yes, I suppose so," said Paul; "but he has to sell it, and make a profit."

"He could do that, and yet make a profit. I will pay you two hundred and seventy-five dollars, myself—that is, on one condition."

"I don't object to getting twenty-five dollars more," said Paul. "What is the condition?"

"I have an order from a gentleman for a diamond ring for a young lady—an engagement ring, in short. If this suits him, as I think it will, I will pay you what I said. I can easily get three hundred and twenty-five from him."

"How are you going to find out whether it will suit him?"

"Easily. He is stopping at the same hotel with me."

"What hotel is that?"

"Lovejoy's. If you can spare the time and will come with me now, we can arrange matters at once. By the way, you can refer me to some responsible citizen, who will guarantee you. Not, of course, that I have any doubts, but we business men are forced to be cautious."

Paul mentioned Mr. Preston's name.

"Quite satisfactory," answered the jeweler. "I know Mr. Preston personally, and as I am pressed for time, I will accept his name without calling upon him. What is your name?"

"Paul Hoffman."

"I will note it down."

The gentleman from Syracuse drew out a memorandum book, in which he entered Paul's name.

"When you see Mr. Preston, just mention my name; Felix Montgomery."

"I will do so."

"Say, if you please, that I would have called upon him, but, coming to the city strictly on business, was too hurried to do so."

This also Paul promised, and counted himself fortunate in falling in with a friend, or, at all events, acquaintance of Mr. Preston, since he was likely to make twenty-five dollars more than he would otherwise have done.

When he got out of the car at the Astor House, the stranger said:

"It will be half an hour before I can reach Lovejoy's, as I have a business call to make first. Can you call there, say, in three-quarters of an hour?"

"Yes, sir."

"Very well, then, I will expect you. Inquire for me at the desk, and ask the servant to conduct you to my room—you remember my name?"

"Yes, sir—Mr. Felix Montgomery."

"Quite right. Good-by, then, till we meet."

The Astor House, which is mentioned several times in the story.

Mr. Felix Montgomery went into the Astor House, and remained about five minutes. He then came out on the steps, and, looking about him to see if Paul was anywhere near, descended the steps, and walked across to Lovejoy's Hotel. Going up to the desk, he inquired:

"Can you accommodate me with a room?"

"Yes, sir; please enter your name."

The stranger entered his name with a flourish, as Felix Montgomery, Syracuse.

"Room No. 237," said the clerk; "will you go up now?"

"Yes, I think so."

"Any luggage?"

"My trunk will be brought from the St. Nicholas in the course of the afternoon."

"We require payment in advance where there is no luggage."

"Very well. I will pay for one day. I am not sure but I shall get through my business in time to go away to-morrow."

Here the servant appeared to conduct Mr. Montgomery to his room.

"By the way," he said, turning back, as if it were an afterthought, "I directed a boy to call here for me in about half an hour. When he comes you may send him up to my room."

"Very well, sir."

Mr. Montgomery followed the servant upstairs to room No. 237. It was rather high up, but he seemed well pleased that this was the case.

"Hope you won't get tired of climbing, sir," said the servant.

"No—I've got pretty good wind."

"Most gentlemen complain of going up so far."

"It makes little difference to me."

At length they reached the room, and Mr. Montgomery entered.

"This will answer very well," he said, with a hasty glance about him. "When my trunk comes, I want it sent up."

"Yes, sir."

"I believe that is all; you can go."

The servant retired and Mr. Felix Montgomery sat down upon the bed.

"My little plot seems likely to succeed," he said to himself. "I've been out of luck lately, but this boy's ring will give me a lift. He can't suspect anything. He'll be sure to come."

Probably the reader has already suspected that Mr. Felix Montgomery was not a jeweler from Syracuse, nor had he any claim to the name under which he at present figured. He was a noted confidence man, who lived by preying upon the community. His appearance was in his favor, and it was his practice to assume the dress and air of a respectable middle-aged citizen, as in the present instance. The sight of the diamond ring had excited his cupidity, and he had instantly formed the design of getting possession of it, if possible. Thus far, his plan promised success.

Meanwhile, Paul loitered away the time in the City Hall Park for half an hour or more. He did not care to go home until his negotiation was complete, and he could report the ring sold, and carry home the money.

"Won't mother be astonished," he thought, "at the price I got for the ring? I'm in luck this morning."

When the stipulated time had passed, Paul rose from the bench on which he was seated, and walked to Lovejoy's Hotel, not far distant.

"Has Mr. Felix Montgomery a room here?" he asked.

"Yes," answered the clerk. "Did you wish to see him?"

"Yes, sir."

"He mentioned that a boy would call by appointment. Here, James, show this boy up to No. 237—Mr. Montgomery's room."

A hotel servant appeared, and Paul followed him up several flights of stairs till they stood before No. 237.

"This is the room, sir," said James. "Wait a minute, and I'll knock."

In answer to the knock, Mr. Montgomery himself opened the door.

"Come in," he said to Paul; "I was expecting you."

So Paul, not suspecting treachery, entered No. 237.

A trolley car, much like the one where Felix Montgomery overheard Paul telling George Barry about the ring.

CHAPTER XVIII

A CLEVER THIEF

"Take a seat," said Mr. Montgomery. "My friend will be in directly. Meanwhile will you let me look at the ring once more?"

Paul took it from his pocket, and handed it to the jeweler from Syracuse, as he supposed him to be.

Mr. Montgomery took it to the window, and appeared to be examining it carefully.

He stood with his back to Paul, but this did not excite suspicion on the part of our hero.

"I am quite sure," he said, still standing with his back to Paul, "that this will please my friend. From the instructions he gave me, it is precisely what he wanted."

While uttering these words, he had drawn a sponge and a vial of chloroform from his side pocket. He saturated the former from the vial, and then, turning quickly, seized Paul, too much taken by surprise to make immediate resistance, and applied the sponge to his nose. When he realized that foul play was meditated, he began to struggle, but he was in a firm grasp, and the chloroform was already beginning to do its work. His head began to swim, and he was speedily in a state of insensibility. When this was accomplished, Mr. Felix Montgomery, eyeing the insensible boy with satisfaction, put on his hat, walked quickly to the door, which he locked on the outside, and made his way rapidly downstairs. Leaving the key at the desk, he left the hotel and disappeared.

Meanwhile Paul slowly recovered consciousness. As he came to himself, he looked about him bewildered, not at first comprehending where he was. All at once it flashed upon him, and he jumped up eagerly and rushed to the door. He tried in vain to open it.

"I am regularly trapped!" he thought, with a feeling of mingled anger and vexation. "What a fool I was to let myself be swindled so easily! I wonder how long I have been lying here insensible?"

Paul was not a boy to give up easily. He meant to get back the ring if it was a possible thing. The first thing was, of course, to get out of his present confinement. He was not used to hotel arrangements and never thought of the bell, but, as the only thing he could think of, began to pound upon the door. But it so happened that at this time there were no servants on that floor, and his appeals

---

93

for help were not heard. Every moment that he had to wait seemed at least five, for no doubt the man who had swindled him was improving the time to escape to a place of safety. Finding that his blows upon the door produced no effect, he began to jump up and down upon the floor, making, in his heavy boots, a considerable noise.

The room directly under No. 237 was occupied by an old gentleman of a very nervous and irascible temper, Mr. Samuel Piper, a country merchant, who, having occasion to be in the city on business for a few days, had put up at Lovejoy's Hotel. He had fatigued himself by some business calls, and was now taking a little rest upon the bed, when he was aroused from half-sleep by the pounding overhead.

"I wish people would have the decency to keep quiet," he said to himself, peevishly. "How can I rest with such a confounded racket going on above!"

He lay back, thinking the noise would cease, but Paul, finding the knocking on the door ineffectual, began to jump up and down, as I have already said. Of course this noise was heard distinctly in the room below.

"This is getting intolerable!" exclaimed Mr. Piper, becoming more and more excited. "The man ought to be indicted as a common nuisance. How they can allow such goings-on in a respectable hotel, I can't understand. I should think the fellow was splitting wood upstairs."

He took his cane, and, standing on the bed, struck it furiously against the ceiling, intending it as signal to the man above to desist. But Paul, catching the response, began to jump more furiously than ever, finding that he had attracted attention.

Mr. Piper became enraged.

"The man must be a lunatic or overcome by drink," he exclaimed. "I can't and I won't stand it."

But the noise kept on.

Mr. Piper put on his shoes and his coat, and, seizing his cane, emerged upon the landing. He espied a female servant just coming upstairs.

"Here, you Bridget, or Nancy, or whatever your name is," he roared, "there's a lunatic upstairs, making a tremendous row in the room over mine. If you don't stop him I'll leave the hotel. Hear him now!"

Bridget let fall her duster in fright.

"Is it a crazy man?" she asked.

"Of course he must be. I want you to go up and stop him."

"Is it me that would go near a crazy man?" exclaimed Bridget, horror-struck; "I wouldn't do it for a million dollars; no, I wouldn't."

"I insist upon your going up," said Mr. Piper, irritably. "He must be stopped. Do you think I am going to stand such an infernal thumping over my head?"

"I wouldn't do it if you'd go down on your knees to me," said Bridget, fervently.

"Come along, I'll go with you."

But the terrified girl would not budge.

"Then you go down and tell your master there's a madman up here. If you don't, I will."

This Bridget consented to do; and, going downstairs, gave a not very coherent account of the disturbance. Three male servants came back with her.

"Is that the man?" asked the first, pointing to Mr. Piper, who certainly looked half wild with irritation.

"Yes," said Bridget, stupidly.

Immediately Mr. Piper found himself pinioned on either side by a stout servant.

"What have you been kickin' up a row for?" demanded the first.

"Let me alone, or I'll have the law take care of you," screamed the outraged man. "Can't you hear the fellow that's making the racket?"

Paul, tired with thumping, had desisted for a moment, but now had recommenced with increased energy. The sounds could be distinctly heard on the floor below.

"Excuse me, sir. I made a mistake," said the first speaker, releasing his hold. "We'll go up and see what's the matter."

So the party went upstairs, followed at a distance by Bridget, who, influenced alike by fear and curiosity, did not know whether to go up or retreat.

The sounds were easily traced to room No. 237. In front of this, therefore, the party congregated.

"What's the matter in there?" asked James, the first servant, putting his lips to the keyhole.

"Yes," chimed in Mr. Piper, irritably; "what do you mean by such an infernal hubbub?"

95

"Open the door, and let me out," returned Paul, eagerly.

The party looked at each other in surprise. They did not expect to find the desperate maniac a boy.

"Perhaps there's more than one of them," suggested the second servant, prudently.

"Why don't you come out yourself?" asked James. "I am locked in."

The door was opened with a passkey and Paul confronted the party.

"Now, young man, what do you mean by making such a disturbance?" demanded Mr. Piper, excitably. "My room is just below, and I expected every minute you would come through."

"I am sorry if I disturbed you, sir," said Paul, politely; "but it was the only way I could attract attention."

"How came you locked up here?"

"Yes," chimed in James, suspiciously, "how came you locked up here?"

"I was drugged with chloroform, and locked in," said Paul.

"Who did it?"

"Mr. Felix Montgomery; or that's what he called himself. I came here by appointment to meet him."

"What did he do that for?"

"He has carried off a diamond ring which I came up here to sell him."

"A very improbable story," said Mr. Piper, suspiciously. "What should such a boy have to do with a diamond ring?"

Nothing is easier than to impart suspicion. Men are prone to believe evil of each other; and Paul was destined to realize this. The hotel servants, ignorant and suspicious, caught the suggestion.

"It's likely he's a' thafe," said Bridget, from a safe distance.

"If I were," said Paul, coolly, "I shouldn't be apt to call your attention by such a noise. I can prove to you that I am telling the truth. I stopped at the office, and the bookkeeper sent a servant to show me up here."

"If this is true," said Mr. Piper, "why, when you found yourself locked in, didn't you ring the bell, instead of making such a confounded racket? My nerves won't get over it for a week."

"I didn't think of the bell," said Paul; "I am not much used to hotels."

"What will we do with him?" asked James, looking to Mr. Piper for counsel.

"You'd better take him downstairs, and see if his story is correct," said the nervous gentleman, with returning good sense.

"I'll do it," said James, to whom the very obvious suggestion seemed marked by extraordinary wisdom, and he grasped Paul roughly by the arm.

"You needn't hold me," said our hero, shaking off the grasp. "I haven't any intention of running away. I want to find out, if I can, what has become of the man that swindled me."

James looked doubtfully at Mr. Piper.

"I don't think he means to run away," said that gentleman. "I begin to think his story is correct. And hark you, my young friend, if you ever get locked up in a hotel room again, just see if there is a bell before you make such a confounded racket."

"Yes, sir, I will," said Paul, half-smiling; "but I'll take care not to get locked up again. It won't be easy for anybody to play that trick on me again."

The party filed downstairs to the office and Paul told his story to the bookkeeper.

"Have you seen Mr. Montgomery go out?" asked our hero.

"Yes, he went out half an hour ago, or perhaps more. He left his key at the desk, but said nothing. He seemed to be in a hurry."

"You didn't notice in what direction he went?"

"No."

Of course no attempt was made to detain Paul. There could be no case against him. He went out of the hotel, and looked up and down Broadway in a state of indecision. He did not mean to sit down passively and submit to the swindle. But he had no idea in what direction to search for Mr. Felix Montgomery.

—

97

CHAPTER XIX

PAUL DELIBERATES

Paul stood in the street irresolute. He looked hopelessly up and down Broadway, but of course the jeweler from Syracuse was not to be seen. Seeking for him in a city containing hundreds of streets and millions of inhabitants was about as discouraging as hunting for a needle in a haystack. But difficult as it was, Paul was by no means ready to give up the search. Indeed, besides the regret he felt at the loss, he was mortified at having been so easily outwitted.

"He's taken me in just as if I was a country boy," thought Paul. "I dare say he's laughing at me now. I'd like to get even with him."

Finally he decided to go to Tiffany's, and ask them to detain any one who might bring in the ring and offer it for sale. He at once acted upon this thought, and, hailing a Broadway stage, for no time was to be lost, soon reached his destination. Entering the store, he walked up to the counter and addressed the clerk to whom he had before shown the ring.

"Do you remember my offering you a diamond ring for sale this morning?" he asked.

"Yes, I remember it very well. Have you got it with you?"

"No, it has been stolen from me."

"Indeed! How was that?" asked the clerk, with interest.

"I met in the cars a well-dressed man, who called himself a jeweler from Syracuse. He examined the ring, and offered me more than Mr. Tiffany, but asked me to bring it to him at Lovejoy's Hotel. When I got there, he drugged me with chloroform, and when I recovered he was gone."

"You have been unlucky. There are plenty of such swindlers about. You should have been careful about displaying the ring before strangers."

"I was showing it to a friend."

"Have you notified the police?"

"Not yet. I came here to let you know, because I thought the thief might bring it in here to sell."

"Very likely. Give me a description of him."

Paul described Mr. Felix Montgomery to the best of his ability.

"I think I should know him from your description. I will speak to Mr. Tiffany, and he will no doubt give orders to detain any person who may offer the ring for sale."

"Thank you."

"If you will give me your address, we will notify you in case the ring is brought in."

Paul left his address, and went out of the store, feeling that he had taken one step toward the recovery of his treasure. He next visited the police headquarters, and left a detailed description of the man who had relieved him of the ring and of the circumstances attending the robbery. Then he went home.

His mother looked up as he entered.

"Well, Paul?" she said, inquiringly.

"I've got bad news, mother," he said.

"What is it? Tell me quick!" she said, nervously.

"The ring has been stolen from me."

"How did it happen, Paul?"

"First, I must tell you how much the ring is worth. I went up to Tiffany's, and showed the ring to Mr. Tiffany himself. He told me that he would give me two hundred and fifty dollars for it, if I would satisfy him that I had a right to sell it."

"Two hundred and fifty dollars!" repeated Mrs. Hoffman, in amazement.

"Yes, the diamond is very large and pure."

"Two hundred and fifty dollars would be a great help to us."

"Yes, mother, that is what makes me feel so bad about being swindled out of it."

"Tell me how it happened. Is there no chance of recovering it?"

"A little. I shall do what I can. I have already notified the police, and Mr. Tiffany."

"You have not told me yet how you lost it."

When Paul had told the story, his mother asked, "Did you mention it in the cars that you had offered it at Tiffany's?"

"Yes, and I mentioned his offer."

"Perhaps the thief would be cautious about going there, for that very reason. He might think the ring would be recognized."

"He would go to a large place, thinking that so valuable a ring would be more readily purchased there."

"He might go to Ball & Black's."

"That is true."

"It would be well to give notice there also."

"I will go up there at once. I only wish I could meet Mr. Felix Montgomery; I don't think he would find it so easy to outreach me a second time."

"Take some dinner first, Paul."

"Then I must hurry it down, mother; I don't want to run the risk of getting too late to Ball & Black's. I can't help thinking what a splendid thing it would be if we had the two hundred and fifty dollars. I would buy out Barry's stand, and I would get a sewing-machine for you, and we could live much more comfortably. It makes me mad to think I let that villain take me in so! He must think me jolly green."

"Anybody might have been deceived, Paul. You mustn't blame yourself too much for that."

Leaving Paul on his way to Ball & Black's, we return to Mr. Felix Montgomery, as we shall continue to call him, though he had no right to the name. After stupefying Paul, as already described, he made his way downstairs, and, leaving his key at the desk, went out.

"I hope my young friend will enjoy himself upstairs," he chuckled to himself. "He's quite welcome to the use of the room till to-morrow morning. It's paid for in advance, and I don't think I shall find it convenient to stop there."

He took the ring from his vest pocket and glanced at it furtively.

"It's a beauty," he murmured, complacently. "I never saw a handsomer ring of the size. What was it the boy said he was offered for it? Two hundred and fifty dollars! That'll give me a lift, and it doesn't come any too soon. My money is pretty low."

He walked across the City Hall Park, and at Barclay Street entered a University place car.

"Evenin' paper, mister?" said a ragged newsboy, whose garments were constructed on the most approved system of ventilation.

"What have you got?"

"Evenin' Post, Mail, Express!"

"Give me an Express. Here's ten cents."

"I haven't got but three cents change, mister."

"Never mind the change," said Mr. Montgomery, in a fit of temporary generosity, occasioned by his good luck.

"Thank you, sir," said the newsboy, regarding Mr. Montgomery as a philanthropist worthy of his veneration.

Felix Montgomery leaned back in his seat, and, with a benevolent smile, ran his eyes over the columns of the Express. Among the paragraphs which attracted his attention was one relating to a comrade, of similar profession, who had just been arrested in Albany while in the act of relieving a gentleman of his pocketbook.

"Jerry always was a bungler," said Mr. Montgomery, complacently, to himself. "He can't hold a candle to me. I flatter myself that I know how to manage a little affair, like this, for instance, as well as the next man. It'll take a sharp detective to lay hold of me."

It might have been thought that the manner in which he had gained possession of the ring would have troubled Mr. Montgomery, but it was many years since he had led an honest life. He had made a living by overreaching others, and his conscience had become so blunted as to occasion him little trouble. He appeared to think that the world owed him a living, and that he was quite justified in collecting the debt in any way he could.

About twenty minutes brought the car to Amity Street and Mr. Montgomery signaled the conductor, and, the car being stopped, he got out.

He walked a few rods in a westerly direction, and paused before a three-story brick house, which appeared to have seen better days.

It was now used as a boarding, or rather lodging-house. The guests were not of a very high character, the landlady not being particular as long as her rent was paid regularly. Mr. Montgomery ascended the steps in a jaunty way, and, opening the door with a passkey, ascended the front staircase. He paused before a room on the third floor, and knocked in a peculiar manner.

The door was opened by a tall woman, in rather neglected attire.

"So you're back," she said.

"Yes, my dear, home again. As the poet says, 'There is no place like home.'"

"I should hope there wasn't," said Mrs. Montgomery, looking about her disdainfully. "A very delightful home it makes with such a charming prospect of the back yard. I've been moping here all day."

"You've found something to console you, I see," said her husband, glancing at the table, on which might be seen a bottle of brandy, half-emptied, and a glass.

101

"Yes," said Mrs. Montgomery; "I felt so bad I had to send out for something. It took every cent I had. And, by the way, Mrs. Flagg sent in her bill, this morning, for the last two weeks' board; she said she must have it."

"My dear," said Mr. Montgomery, "she shall have it."

"You don't mean to say you've got the money, Tony!" exclaimed his wife, in surprise.

"No, I haven't got the money; but I've got what's just as good."

"What have you got?"

"What do you say to this?" and Mr. Montgomery drew from his pocket the diamond ring, whose loss was so deeply felt by our hero.

"Is that genuine?" asked the lady.

"It's the real thing."

"What a beauty! Where did you get it?"

"It was kindly presented me by a young man of the tender age of fifteen or thereabouts, who had no further use for it."

"You did him out of it, that is. Tell me how you did it."

Mr. Montgomery told the story. His wife listened with interest and appreciation.

"That was a smart operation, Tony," she said.

"I should say it was, Maria."

"How much is the ring worth?"

"Two hundred and fifty dollars."

"Can you get that for it?"

"I can get that for it."

"Tony, you are a treasure."

"Have you just found that out, my dear?"

CHAPTER XX

THE THIEF IN DISGUISE

It will be inferred, from the preceding conversation, that Mrs. Montgomery was not likely to be shocked by the lack of honesty in her husband. Her conscience was as elastic as his; and she was perfectly willing to help him spend his unlawful gains.

"How soon are you going to sell the ring?" she asked.

"I should like to dispose of it at once, Maria."

"You will need to. Mrs. Flagg wants her bill paid at once."

"I quite understand the necessity of promptness, my dear. Only, you know, one has to be cautious about disposing of articles obtained in this way."

"You say you left the boy locked up. It seems to me, you'd better sell the ring before he has a chance to get out and interfere."

"I don't know but you're right, my dear. Well, we'll get ready."

"Do you want me to go with you?"

"Yes; it will disarm suspicion if you are with me. I think I'll go as a country parson."

"Country parsons are not apt to have diamond rings to dispose of."

"Very true, my dear. The remark does credit to your good judgment and penetration. But I know how to get over that."

"As how?"

"Be a little more particular about your speech, my dear. Remember, you are a minister's wife, and must use refined expressions. What is easier than to say that the ring was given me by a benevolent lady of my congregation, to dispose of for the benefit of the poor?"

"Well thought of, Tony. You've got a good head-piece."

"You're right, my dear. I don't like to indulge in self-praise, but I believe I know a thing or two. And now for the masquerade. Where are the duds?"

"In the black trunk."

"Then we'd better lose no time in putting them on."

Without describing the process of transformation in detail, it will be sufficient to say that the next twenty minutes wrought a decided change in the appearance of Mr. and Mrs. Felix Montgomery. The former was arrayed in a suit of canonical black, not of the latest cut. A white neckcloth was substituted for the more gaudy article worn by the jeweler from Syracuse, and a pair of silver-bowed spectacles, composed of plain glass, lent a scholarly air to his face. His hair was combed behind his ears, and, so far as appearance went, he quite looked the character of a clergyman from the rural districts.

"How will I do, my dear?" he asked, complacently.

"Tiptop," answered the lady. "How do I look?"

Mrs. Montgomery had put on a dress of sober tint, and scant circumference, contrasting in a marked manner with the mode then prevailing. A very plain collar encircled her neck. Her hands were incased in brown silk gloves, while her husband wore black kids. Her bonnet was exceedingly plain, and her whole costume was almost Quaker-like in its simplicity.

Her husband surveyed her with satisfaction.

"My dear," he said, "you are a fitting helpmeet for the Rev. Mr. Barnes, of Hayfield Centre. By Jove, you do me credit!"

"'By Jove' is not a proper expression for a man of your profession, Mr. Barnes," said the new minister's wife, with a smile.

"You are right, my dear. I must eschew profanity, and cultivate a decorous style of speech. Well, are we ready?"

"I am."

"Then let us set forth on our pilgrimage. We will imagine, Mrs. Barnes, that we are about to make some pastoral calls."

They emerged into the street. On the way downstairs they met Mrs. Flagg, the landlady, who bowed respectfully. She was somewhat puzzled, however, not knowing when they were let in.

"Good-morning, madam," said Mr. Barnes. "Are you the landlady of this establishment?"

"Yes, sir."

"I have been calling on one of your lodgers—Mr. Anthony Blodgett (this was the name by which Mr. Felix Montgomery was known in the house). He is a very worthy man."

Now, to tell the truth, Mrs. Flagg had not been particularly struck by the moral worth of her lodger, and this testimony led her to entertain doubts as to the discernment of her clerical visitor.

"You know him, then?"

"I know him as myself, madam. Have you never heard him mention the name of Rev. Mr. Barnes, of Hayfield Centre, Connecticut?"

"I can't say I have," answered the landlady.

"That is singular. We were always very intimate. We attended the same school as boys, and, in fact, were like Damon and Pythias."

Mrs. Flagg had never heard of Damon and Pythias, still she understood the comparison.

"You're in rather a different line now," she remarked, dryly.

"Yes, our positions are different. My friend dwells in the busy metropolis, while I pass a quiet, peaceful existence in a secluded country village, doing what good I can. But, my dear, we are perhaps detaining this worthy lady from her domestic avocations. I think we must be going."

"Very well, I am ready."

The first sound of her voice drew the attention of the landlady. Mrs. Felix Montgomery possessed a thin somewhat shrill, voice, which she was unable to conceal, and, looking attentively at her, Mrs. Flagg penetrated her disguise. Then, turning quickly to the gentleman, aided by her new discovery, she also recognized him.

"Well, I declare," said she, "if you didn't take me in beautifully."

Mr. Montgomery laughed heartily.

"You wouldn't know me, then?" he said.

"You're got up excellent," said Mrs. Flagg, with a slight disregard for grammar. "Is it a joke?"

"Yes, a little practical joke. We're going to call on some friends and see if they know us."

"You'd do for the theatre," said the landlady, admiringly.

"I flatter myself I might have done something on the stage, if my attention had been turned that way. But, my dear, we must be moving, or we shan't get through our calls."

"I wonder what mischief they are up to now," thought Mrs. Flagg, as she followed them to the door. "I know better than to think they'd take the trouble to dress up that way just to take in their friends. No, they're up to some game. Not that I care, as long as they get money enough to pay my bill."

So the worldly-wise landlady dismissed them from her thoughts, and went about her work.

Mr. Barnes and his wife walked up toward Broadway at a slow, decorous pace, suited to the character they had assumed. More than one who met them turned back to look at what they considered a perfect type of the country minister and his wife. They would have been not a little surprised to learn that under this quiet garb walked two of the most accomplished swindlers in a city abounding in adventurers of all kinds.

Mr. Barnes paused a moment to reprove a couple of urchins who were pitching pennies on the sidewalk.

"Don't you know that it's wrong to pitch pennies?" he said gravely.

"None of your chaff, mister," retorted one of the street boys, irreverently. "When did you come from the country, old Goggles?"

"My son, you should address me with more respect."

"Just get out of the way, mister! I don't want to hear no preachin'."

"I am afraid you have been badly brought up, my son."

"I ain't your son, and I wouldn't be for a shillin'. Just you go along, and let me alone!"

"A sad case of depravity, my dear," remarked Mr. Barnes to his wife. "I fear we must leave these boys to their evil ways."

"You'd better," said one of the boys.

"They're smart little rascals!" said Mr. Montgomery, when they were out of hearing of the boys. "I took them in, though. They thought I was the genuine article."

"We'd better not waste any more time," said his wife. "That boy might get out, you know, and give us trouble."

"I don't believe he will get out in a hurry. I locked the door and he'd have to pound some time before he could make any one hear, I declare, I should like to see how he looked when he recovered from his stupor, and realized that his ring was gone."

"What sort of boy was he, Tony?"

"Better not call me by that name, my dear. It might be heard, you know, and might not be considered in character. As to your question, he was by no means a stupid boy. Rather sharpish, I should say."

"Then how came he to let you take him in?"

"As to that, I claim to be rather sharp myself, and quite a match even for a smart boy. I haven't knocked about the world forty-four years for nothing."

They were now in Broadway. Turning the corner of Amity Street, they walked a short distance downtown, and paused before the handsome jewelry store of Ball & Black.

"I think we had better go in here," said Felix Montgomery—(I hesitate a little by which of his numerous names to call him).

"Why not go to Tiffany's?"

"I gather from what the boy told me that the ring has already been offered there. It would be very likely to be recognized and that would be awkward, you know."

"Are you sure the ring has not been offered here? asked his wife.

"Quite sure. The boy would have mentioned it, had such been the case."

"Very well. Let us go in then."

The Rev. Mr. Barnes and his wife, of Hayfield Centre; entered the elegant store, and ten minutes later Paul Hoffman entered also, and took his station at the counters wholly unconscious of the near proximity of the man who had so artfully swindled him.

CHAPTER XXI

PAUL IS CHECKMATED

On entering the large jewelry store Mr. Montgomery and his wife walked to the rear of the store, and advanced to the counter, behind which stood a clerk unengaged.

"What shall I show you?" he inquired

"I didn't come to purchase," said Mr. Montgomery, with suavity, "but to sell. I suppose you purchase jewelry at times?"

"Sometimes," said the clerk. "Let me see what you have."

"First," said the adventurer, "let me introduce myself. I am the Rev. Mr. Barnes, of Hayfield Centre, Connecticut. You perhaps know the place?"

"I don't think I remember it," said the clerk, respectfully.

"It is a small place," said Mr. Montgomery, modestly, "but my tastes are plain and unobtrusive, and I do not aspire to a more conspicuous post. However, that is not to the purpose. A lady parishioner, desiring to donate a portion of her wealth to the poor, has placed in my hand a diamond ring, the proceeds to be devoted to charitable objects. I desire to sell it, and, knowing the high reputation of your firm feel safe in offering it to you. I know very little of the value of such things, since they are not in my line, but I am sure of fair treatment at your hands."

"You may depend upon that," said the clerk, favorably impressed with the appearance and manners of his customer. "Allow me to see the ring."

The brilliant was handed over the counter.

"It is quite valuable," said he, scrutinizing it closely.

"So I supposed, as the lady is possessed of wealth. You may rely upon its being genuine."

"I am not authorized to purchase," said the clerk, "but I will show it to one of the firm."

Just at that moment, Mr. Montgomery, chancing to look toward the door, was startled by seeing the entrance of Paul Hoffman. He saw that it would be dangerous to carry the negotiation any further and he quickly gave a secret signal to his wife.

The hint was instantly understood and acted upon.

Mrs. Montgomery uttered a slight cry, and clung to her husband's arm.

"My dear," she said, "I feel one of my attacks coming on. Take me out quickly.

"My wife is suddenly taken sick," said Mr. Montgomery, hurriedly.

"She is subject to fits. If you will give me the ring, I will return to-morrow and negotiate for its sale."

"I am very sorry," said the clerk, with sympathy, handing back the ring. "Can I get anything for the lady?"

"No, thank you. The best thing to do is to get her into the open air. Thank you for your kindness."

"Let me help you," said the clerk, and coming from behind the counter he took one arm of Mrs. Montgomery, who, leaning heavily on her husband and the clerk, walked, or rather was carried, to the street door.

Of course, the attention of all within the store was drawn to the party.

"What was the matter?" inquired a fellow-clerk, as the salesman returned.

"It was a clergyman from Connecticut, who wished to sell a diamond ring, given to him for charitable purposes. His wife was taken suddenly sick. He will bring it back to-morrow."

"Was the ring a valuable one?"

"It must be worth in the neighborhood of three hundred dollars."

Paul listened to this explanation, and a sudden light flashed upon him, as he heard the estimated value of the ring. There had been something familiar in the appearance of the adventurer, though, on account of his successful disguise and his being accompanied by a lady, he had not before felt any suspicion as to his identity with the man who had swindled him. Now he felt convinced that it was Mr. Felix Montgomery, and that it was his own appearance which had led to the sudden sickness and the precipitate departure.

"That trick won't work, Mr. Montgomery," he said to himself. "I've got on your track sooner than I anticipated, and I mean to follow you up."

Reaching the sidewalk, he caught sight of Mr. and Mrs. Montgomery just turning the corner of a side street. The pair supposed they were safe, not thinking that our hero had recognized them, and the lady no longer exhibited illness, and was walking briskly at her husband's side. Paul hurried up and tapped the adventurer on the shoulder. Mr. Montgomery, turning, was annoyed on finding that he had not yet escaped. He determined, however, to stick to his false character, and deny all knowledge of the morning's transaction.

"Well, my young friend," he said, "do you want me? I believe I have not the pleasure of your acquaintance."

"You are mistaken there, Mr. Felix Montgomery," said Paul, significantly.

"By what name did you address me?" said the swindler, assuming a tone of surprise.

"I addressed you as Mr. Felix Montgomery."

"You have made a mistake, my good friend. I am an humble clergyman from Connecticut. I am called the Rev. Mr. Barnes. Should you ever visit Hayfield Centre, I shall be glad to receive a call from you."

"When I last met you, you were a jeweler from Syracuse," said Paul, bluntly.

Mr. Montgomery laughed heartily.

"My dear," he said, turning to his wife, "is not this an excellent joke? My young friend here thinks he recognizes in me a jeweler from Syracuse."

"Indeed, you are quite mistaken," said the lady. "My husband is a country minister. We came up to the city this morning on a little business."

"I understand on what business," said Paul. "You wanted to dispose of a diamond ring."

Mr. Montgomery was disposed to deny the charge, but a moment's reflection convinced him that it would be useless, as Paul had doubtless been informed in Ball & Black's of his business there. He decided to put on a bold front and admit it.

"I suppose you were in Ball & Black's just now," he said.

"I was."

"And so learned my business there? But I am at a loss to understand why you should be interested in the matter."

"That ring is mine," said Paul. "You swindled me out of it this morning."

"My young friend, you must certainly be insane," said Mr. Montgomery, shrugging his shoulders. "My dear, did you hear that?"

"He is an impudent boy," said the lady. "I am surprised that you should be willing to talk to him."

"If you leave here I will put a policeman on your track," said Paul.

He looked so determined that Mr. Montgomery found that he must parley.

"You are under a strange hallucination, my young friend," he said. "If you will walk along with me, I think I can convince you of your mistake."

"There is no mistake about the matter," said Paul, walking on with them. "The ring is mine, and I must have it."

"My dear, will you explain about the ring? He may credit your testimony."

"I don't see that any explanation is necessary," said the lady. "However, since you wish it, I will say that the ring was handed you by Mrs. Benton, a wealthy lady of your parish, with instructions to sell it, and devote the proceeds to charitable purposes."

"Is that explanation satisfactory?" asked Mr. Montgomery.

"No, it is not," said Paul, resolutely. "I don't believe one word of it. I recognize you in spite of your dress. You gave me chloroform this morning in a room in Lovejoy's Hotel, and when I was unconscious you made off with the ring which I expected to sell you. You had better return it, or I will call a policeman."

"I am not the person you take me for," said Felix Montgomery.

"You are the jeweler from Syracuse who swindled me out of my ring."

"I never was a jeweler, and never lived in Syracuse," said the adventurer, with entire truth.

"You may be right, but that is what you told me this morning."

"I wish you would go away, and cease to annoy us," said the lady, impatiently.

"I want my ring."

"We have no ring of yours."

"Show me the ring, and if it is not mine I will go away."

"You are a very impudent fellow, upon my word," said Mrs. Montgomery, sharply, "to accuse a gentleman like my husband of taking your ring. I don't believe you ever had one."

"My dear," interposed her husband, mildly, "I dare say my young friend here really thinks we have his ring. Of course it is a great mistake. Imagine what our friends in Hayfield Centre would think of such a charge! But you must remember that he is unacquainted with my standing in the community. In order to satisfy his mind, I am willing to let him see the ring."

"To let him see the ring?" repeated the lady, in surprise.

"Yes. Here, my lad," taking the ring from his pocket, "this is the ring. You will see at once that it is not yours."

"I see that it is mine," said Paul, taking the proffered ring, and preparing to go, astonished at his own good fortune in so easily recovering it.

"Not so fast!" exclaimed Mr. Montgomery, seizing him by the shoulder. "Help! Police!"

An officer had turned the corner just before, and it was this that had suggested the trap. He came up quickly, and, looking keenly from one to the other, inquired what was the matter.

"This boy has just purloined a ring from my wife," said Mr. Montgomery. "Fortunately I caught him in the act."

"Give up the ring, you young scoundrel!" said the officer, imposed upon by the clerical appearance of the adventurer.

"It is mine," said Paul.

"None of your gammon! Give up the ring, and come with me."

The ring was restored to Mr. Montgomery, who overwhelmed the officer with a profusion of thanks.

"It is not a diamond, only an imitation," he said, "but my wife values it as the gift of a friend. Don't be too hard on the boy. He may not be so bad as he seems."

"I'll attend to him," said the policeman, emphatically. "I'll learn him to rob ladies of rings in the street. Come along, sir!"

Paul tried to explain matters, but no attention was paid to his protestations. To his anger and mortification he saw the swindler make off triumphantly with the ring, while he, the wronged owner, was arrested as a thief.

But at the station-house he had his revenge. He was able to prove to his captor that he had lodged information against Mr. Montgomery, and the policeman in turn was mortified to think how readily he had been imposed upon. Of course Paul was set free, but the officer's blundering interference seemed to render the recovery of the ring more doubtful than ever.

CHAPTER XXII

A MAN OF RESOURCES

"Well, that was a narrow escape," said Mr. Montgomery, with a sigh of relief. "I think I managed rather cleverly, eh?"

"I wanted to box the boys ears," said Mrs. Montgomery, sharply.

"It wouldn't have been in character, my dear. Ha, ha!" he laughed, softly, "we imposed upon the officer neatly. Our young friend got rather the worst of it."

"Why don't you call things by their right names? He isn't much of a friend."

"Names are of no consequence, my dear."

"Well, what are you going to do next?" asked the lady, abruptly.

"About the ring?"

"Of course."

"I hardly know," said Mr. Montgomery, reflectively. "If it were not for appearing too anxious, I would go back to Ball & Black's now that our young friend is otherwise engaged, and can't interrupt us."

"Suppose we go?"

"Well, you see, it might be considered rather soon for you to recover from your fit. Besides, I don't know what stories this boy may have thought fit to tell about us."

"He didn't have time to say anything."

"Perhaps you are right."

"We want to dispose of the ring as soon as possible, and leave the city."

"That is true. Well, if you say so, we will go back."

"It seems to me now is the best time. The boy will tell his story to the officer and we may be inquired for."

"Then, my dear, I will follow your advice."

Mr. and Mrs. Montgomery turned, and directed their steps again toward Broadway. The distance was short, and fifteen minutes had scarcely elapsed since they left the store before they again entered it. They made their way to the lower end of the store and accosted the same clerk with whom they had before spoken.

"Is your wife better?" he asked.

"Much better, thank you. A turn in the air always relieves her, and she is quite herself again. I have returned because it is necessary for me to leave the city by the evening train, and my time is, therefore, short. Will you be kind enough to show the ring to your employer, and ask him if he will purchase?"

The clerk returned, and said that the firm would pay two hundred and fifty dollars, but must be assured of his right to dispose of it.

"Did you mention my name?" asked the adventurer.

"I mentioned that you were a clergyman. I could not remember the name."

"The Rev. Mr. Barnes, of Hayfield Centre, Connecticut. I have been preaching there for—is it six or seven years, my dear?"

"Seven," said his wife.

"I should think that would be sufficient. You may mention that to Mr. Ball or Mr. Black, if you please. I presume after that he will not be afraid to purchase."

Mr. Montgomery said this with an air of conscious respectability and high standing, which might readily impose upon strangers. But, by bad luck, what he had said was heard by a person able to confute him.

"Did you say you were from Hayfield Centre?" asked a gentleman, standing a few feet distant.

"Yes," said Mr. Montgomery.

"I think you said your name was Barnes?"

"Yes, sir."

"And that you have been preaching there for the last seven years?"

"Yes, sir," answered Mr. Montgomery, but there was rather less confidence in his tone. In fact he was beginning to feel uneasy.

"It is very strange," said the other. "I have a sister living in Hayfield Centre, and frequently visit the place myself, and so of course know something of it. Yet I have never heard of any clergyman named Barnes preaching there."

Mr. Montgomery saw that things looked critical.

"You are strangely mistaken, sir," he said. "However, I will not press the sale. If you will return the ring (to the clerk) I will dispose of it elsewhere."

But the clerk's suspicions had been aroused by what had been said.

"I will first speak to Mr. Ball," he said.

"There is no occasion to speak to him. I shall not sell the ring to-day. To-morrow, I will come with witnesses whose testimony will outweigh that of this gentleman, who I suspect never was in Hayfield Centre in his life. I will trouble you for the ring."

"I hope you don't intend to give it to him," said the gentleman. "The presumption is that, as he is masquerading, he has not come by it honestly."

"I shall not deign to notice your insinuations," said Mr. Montgomery, who concealed beneath a consequential tone his real uneasiness. "The ring, if you please."

"Don't give it to him."

As the clerk seemed disinclined to surrender the ring, Mr. Montgomery said: "Young man, you will find it to be a serious matter to withhold my property."

"Perhaps I had better give it to him," said the clerk, imposed upon by the adventurer's manner.

"Require him to prove property. If it is really his, he can readily do this."

"My dear," said the Rev. Mr. Barnes, "we will leave the store."

"What, and leave the ring?"

"For the present. I will invoke the aid of the police to save me from being robbed in this extraordinary manner."

He walked to the street door, accompanied by his wife. He was deeply disappointed at the failure of the sale, and would gladly have wreaked vengeance upon the stranger who had prevented it. But he saw that his safety required an immediate retreat. In addition to his own disappointment, he had to bear his wife's censure.

"If you had the spirit of a man, Mr. Montgomery," she commenced, "you wouldn't have given up that ring so easily. He had no business to keep it."

"I would have called in a policeman if I dared, but you know I am not on the best of terms with these gentlemen."

"Are we to lose the ring, then?"

"I am afraid so, unless I can make them believe in the store that I am really what I pretend to be."

"Can't you do it?"

"Not very easily, unless stay, I have an idea. Do you see that young man?"

115

He directed his wife's attention to a young man, evidently fresh from the country, who was approaching, staring open-eyed at the unwonted sights of the city. He was dressed in a blue coat with brass buttons, while his pantaloons, of a check pattern, terminated rather higher up than was in accordance with the fashion.

"Yes, I see him," said Mrs. Montgomery. "What of him?"

"I am going to recover the ring through his help."

"I don't see how."

"You will see."

"How do you do?" said the adventurer, cordially, advancing to the young man, and seizing his hand.

"Pretty smart," said the countryman, looking surprised.

"Are your parents quite well?"

"They're so's to be around."

"When did you come to the city?"

"This mornin'."

"Do you stay any length of time?"

"I'm goin' back this afternoon."

"You didn't expect to meet me now, did you?" asked Mr. Montgomery.

"I s'pose I'd orter know you," said the perplexed youth, "but I can't think what your name is."

"What! Not know Mr. Barnes, the minister of Hayfield Centre? Don't you remember hearing me preach for your minister?"

"Seems to me I do," answered the young man, persuading himself that he ought to remember.

"Of course you do. Now, my young friend, I am very glad to have met you."

"So am I," said the other, awkwardly.

"You can do me a favor, if you will."

"Of course, I will," said Jonathan, "if it's anything I can do."

"Yes, you will have no trouble about it. You see, I went into a jeweler's near by to sell a valuable ring, and they wanted to make sure I was really a minister, and not intending to cheat them. If you will go in with me, and say that you have often heard me preach, and that I am the Rev. Mr. Barnes, of Hayfield Centre, I won't mind paying you five dollars for your trouble."

"All right; I'll do it," said the rustic, considering that it would be an unusually easy way of earning a few dollars.

"You'll remember the name, won't you?"

116

"Yes—Parson Barnes, of Hayfield Centre."

"That is right. The store is near by. Walk along with us, and we will be there in five minutes."

CHAPTER XXIII

A NEW EXPEDIENT

"I believe your name is Peck?" said Mr. Montgomery, hazarding a guess.

"No, it's Young, Ephraim Young."

"Of course it is. I remember now, but I am apt to forget names. You said your parents were quite well?"

"Yes, they're pretty smart."

"I am glad to hear it; I have the pleasantest recollections of your excellent father. Let me see, didn't you call there with me once, Mrs. Barnes?"

"Not that I remember."

"You must go with me the next time. I want you to know the parents of our young friend. They are excellent people. Do you go back this afternoon, Mr. Young?"

"Yes, I guess so. You don't know of any sitooation I could get in a store round here, do you?"

"Not at present, but I have some influential friends to whom I will mention your name. Suppose, now, I could obtain a situation for you, how shall I direct the letter letting you know?"

"Just put on the letter 'Ephraim Young.' Everybody in Plainfield knows me."

"So he lives in Plainfield," said Mr. Montgomery to himself. "It's as well to know that." Then aloud: "I won't forget, Mr. Young. What sort of business would you prefer?"

"Any kind that'll pay," said the gratified youth, firmly convinced of his companion's ability to fulfill his promise. "I've got tired of stayin' round home, and I'd like to try York a little while. Folks say it's easy to make money here."

"You are right. If I were a business man, I would come to New York at once. For a smart young man like you it offers a much better opening than a country village."

"That's what I've told dad often," said the rustic, "but he's afraid I wouldn't get nothing to do and he says it's dreadful expensive livin' here."

"So it is expensive, but then you will be better paid than in the country. However, here we are. You won't forget what I told you?"

"No—I'll remember," said the young man.

The reappearance of Mr. Barnes and wife so soon excited some surprise in the store, for it had got around, as such things will, that he was an impostor, and it was supposed that he would not venture to show his face there again. The appearance of his rustic companion likewise attracted attention. Certainly, Mr. Montgomery (it makes little difference what we call him) did not exhibit the slightest appearance of apprehension, but his manner was quite cool and self-possessed. He made his way to that part of the counter attended by the clerk with whom he had before spoken. He observed with pleasure and relief that the man who had questioned his identity with any of the ministers of Hayfield Centre was no longer in the store. This would make the recovery of the ring considerably easier.

"Well, sir," he said, addressing the clerk, "I suppose you did not expect to see me again so soon?"

"No, sir."

"Nor did I expect to be able to return for the ring before to-morrow, not supposing that I could bring witnesses to prove that I was what I represented. But fortunately I met just now a young friend, who can testify to my identity, as he has heard me preach frequently in Plainfield, where he resides. Mr. Young, will you be kind enough to tell this gentleman who I am?"

"Parson Barnes, of Hayfield Centre," said the youth, confidently.

"You have heard me preach, have you not, in Plainfield?"

"Yes," said the young man, fully believing that he was telling the truth.

"And I have called on your parents?"

"Yes."

"I think," said the adventurer, "that will be sufficient to convince you that I am what I appear."

It was hard to doubt, in the face of such evidence. Ephraim Young was so unmistakably from the rural districts that it would have been absurd to suspect him of being an artful city rogue. Besides, Mr. Barnes himself was got up so naturally that all the clerk's doubts vanished at once. He concluded that the customer who had questioned his genuineness must be very much mistaken.

"I ought to apologize to you, sir," he said, "for doubting your word. But in a city like this you know one has to be very careful."

"Of course," said the adventurer, blandly, "I do not blame you in the least. You only did your duty, though it might have cost me some trouble and inconvenience."

"I am sorry, sir."

"No apologies, I beg. It has all turned out right, and your mistake was a natural one. If you will kindly return me the ring, I will defer selling it, I think, till another day."

The clerk brought the ring, which he handed back to Mr. Montgomery. The latter received it with so much the more satisfaction, as he had made up his mind at one time that it was gone irrevocably, and put it away in his waistcoat pocket.

"I had intended to buy some silver spoons," he said, "but it will be necessary to wait until I have disposed of the ring. However, I may as well look at some, eh, Mrs. Barnes?"

"If you like," assented the lady.

So the pair examined some spoons, and fixed upon a dozen, which they said they would return and buy on the next day, and then, with a polite good-by, went out of the store, leaving behind, on the whole, a favorable impression.

Ephraim Young accompanied them out, and walked along beside them in the street. He, too, was in good spirits, for had not his companion promised him five dollars for his services, which he had faithfully rendered? Five dollars to the young man from the rural districts was a very considerable sum of money—quite a nugget, in fact—and he already enjoyed in advance the pleasure which he anticipated of telling his friends at home how easily he had earned such a sum in "York." He walked along beside the adventurer, expecting that he would say something about paying him, but no allusion was made by the adventurer to his promise. Indeed, five dollars was considerably more than he had in his possession. When they reached Amity Street, for they were now proceeding up Broadway, he sought to shake off the young man, whose company he no longer desired.

"This is our way," he said. "I suppose you are going further. I am very glad to have met you, Mr. Young. I hope you will give our regards to your excellent parents;" and he held out his hand in token of farewell.

"Ain't you goin' to pay me that money?" said Ephraim, bluntly, becoming alarmed at the prospect of losing the nugget he had counted on with so much confidence.

"Bless me, I came near forgetting it! I hope you will excuse me," and to Ephraim's delight he drew out his pocketbook. But the prospect of payment was not so bright as the young man supposed.

"I don't think I have a five-dollar bill," said Mr. Montgomery, after an examination of the pocketbook. "Mrs. Montgomery, do you happen to have a five with you?"

"No, I haven't," said the lady, promptly. "I spent all my money shopping this morning."

"That is unfortunate. Our young friend has rendered us such a service I don't like to make him wait for his money."

Ephraim Young looked rather blank at this suggestion.

"Let me see, I have a hundred-dollar bill here," said Mr. Montgomery. "I will go into the next store, and see if I can't get it changed. Mr. Young, will you be kind enough to remain with my wife?"

"Certain," said Ephraim, brightening up.

Mr. Montgomery went into a shop near by, but made no request to have a hundred-dollar bill changed. He was rather afraid that they might comply with his request, which would have subjected him to some embarrassment. He merely inquired if he could use a pen for a moment; request which was readily granted. In less than five minutes he emerged into the street again. Ephraim Young looked toward him eagerly.

"I am sorry to say, my young friend," he remarked, "that I was unable to get my bill changed. I might get it changed at a bank, but the banks are all closed at this hour."

The countryman looked disturbed.

"I am afraid," continued Mr. Montgomery, "I must wait and send you the money in a letter from Hayfield Centre."

"I'd rather have it now," said Ephraim.

"I am sorry to disappoint you," said the adventurer smoothly; "but after all you will only have a day or two to wait. To make up to you for the delay I have decided to send you ten dollars instead of five. Finding I could not change my bill, I wrote a note for the amount, which I will hand you."

Ephraim received the paper, which the other handed him, and read as follows:

NEW YORK, Sept 15, 18—.

Three days from date I promise to pay Mr. Ephraim Young ten dollars.

———

JOTHAM BARNES, of Hayfield Centre.

"How will that do?" asked the adventurer. "By waiting three days you double your money."

"You'll be sure to send it," said Ephraim, doubtfully.

"My young friend, I hope you do not doubt me," said the Rev. Mr. Barnes, impressively.

"I guess it's all right," said Ephraim, "only I thought I might like to spend the money in the city."

"Much better save it up," said the other. "By and by it may come in useful."

Ephraim carefully folded up the note, and deposited it in an immense wallet, the gift of his father. He would have preferred the money which it represented: but three days would soon pass, and the ten dollars would be forwarded to him. He took leave of his new acquaintances, Mr. Montgomery shaking his hand with affectionate warmth, and requesting him to give his best respects to his parents. When Ephraim was out of sight he returned to his wife, with a humorous twinkle in his eye, and said:

"Wasn't that cleverly done, old lady?"

"Good enough!" remarked the lady. "Now you've got the ring back again, what are you going to do with it?"

"That, my dear, is a subject which requires the maturest consideration. I shall endeavor to convert it as soon as possible into the largest possible sum in greenbacks. Otherwise I am afraid our board bill, and the note I have just given to my rural friend, will remain unpaid."

CHAPTER XXIV

MR. MONTGOMERY'S ARREST

Having shaken off his country acquaintance, of whom he had no further need, Mr. Montgomery started to return to his lodgings. On the whole, he was in good spirits, though he had not effected the sale of the ring. But it was still in his possession, and it had a tangible value.

"I am sorry you did not sell the ring," said Mrs. Montgomery.

"So am I," said her husband. "We may have to sell it in some other city."

"We can't leave the city without money."

"That's true," returned her husband, rather taken aback by what was undeniably true.

"We must sell the ring, or raise money on it, in New York."

"I don't know but you are right. The trouble is, there are not many places where they will buy so expensive an article. Besides, they will be apt to ask impertinent questions."

"You might go to a pawnbroker's."

"And get fleeced. If I got a quarter of the value from a pawnbroker, I should be lucky."

"We must do something with it," said Mrs. Montgomery, decidedly.

"Right, my dear. We must get the sinews of war somewhere. Richard will never be himself again till his pocketbook is lined with greenbacks. At present, who steals my purse steals trash."

"Suppose you try Tiffany's?"

"The ring has already been offered there. They might remember it."

"If they do, say that he is your son."

"A good thought," answered the husband. "I will act upon it. But, on the whole, I'll doff this disguise, and assume my ordinary garments. This time, my dear, I shall not need your assistance."

"Well, the sooner it's done the better. That's all I have to say."

"As soon as possible."

Mr. Montgomery returned to his lodgings in Amity Street, and, taking off his clerical garb, appeared in the garb in which we first made his acquaintance. The change was very speedily effected.

"Wish me good luck, Mrs. M.," he said, as he opened the door. "I am going to make another attempt."

"Good luck to you, Tony! Come back soon."

"As soon as my business is completed. If I get the money, we will leave for Philadelphia this evening. You may as well be packing up."

"I am afraid the landlady won't let us carry away our baggage unless we pay our bill."

"Never mind! Pack it up, and we'll run our chance."

Felix Montgomery left the house with the ring carefully deposited in his vest pocket. To judge from his air of easy indifference, he might readily have been taken for a substantial citizen in excellent circumstances; but then appearances are oftentimes deceitful, and they were especially so in the present instance.

He made his way quickly to Broadway, and thence to Tiffany's, at that time not so far uptown as at present. He entered the store with a nonchalant air, and, advancing to the counter, accosted the same clerk to whom Paul had shown the ring earlier in the day.

"I have a valuable ring which I would like to sell," he said. "Will you tell me its value?"

The clerk no sooner took it in his hand than he recognized it.

"I have seen that ring before," he said, looking at Mr. Montgomery keenly.

"Yes," said the latter, composedly; "this morning, wasn't it?"

"Yes."

"My boy brought it in here. I ought not to have sent him, for he came very near losing it on the way home. I thought it best to come with it myself."

This was said so quietly that it was hard to doubt the statement, or would have been if information had not been brought to the store that the ring had been stolen.

"Yes, boys are careless," assented the clerk, not caring to arouse Mr. Montgomery's suspicions. "You wish to sell the ring, I suppose."

"Yes," answered the other; "I don't like to carry a ring of so great value. Several times I have come near having it stolen. Will you buy it?"

"I am not authorized to make the purchase," said the clerk. "I will refer the matter to Mr. Tiffany."

"Very well," said Mr. Montgomery. "I am willing to accept whatever he may pronounce a fair price."

"No doubt," thought the clerk.

He carried the ring to his employer, and quickly explained the circumstances.

"The man is doubtless a thief. He must be arrested," said the jeweler.

"If I go for an officer, he will take alarm."

"Invite him to come into the back part of the shop, and I will protract the negotiation while you summon a policeman."

The clerk returned, and at his invitation Mr. Montgomery walked to the lower end of the store, where he was introduced to the head of the establishment. Sharp though he was, he suspected no plot.

"You are the owner of this ring?" asked Mr. Tiffany.

"Yes, sir," said the adventurer. "It has been in our family for a long time."

"But you wish to sell it now?"

"Yes; I have come near losing it several times, and prefer to dispose of it. What is its value?"

"That requires some consideration. I will examine it closely."

Mr. Montgomery stood with his back to the entrance, waiting patiently, while the jeweler appeared to be engaged in a close examination of the ring. He congratulated himself that no questions had been asked which it might have been difficult for him to answer. He made up his mind that after due examination Mr. Tiffany would make an offer, which he determined in advance to accept, whatever it might be, since he would consider himself fortunate to dispose of it at even two-thirds of its value.

Meanwhile the clerk quietly slipped out of the store, and at a short distance encountered a policeman, upon whom he called for assistance. At the same moment Paul and Mr. Preston came up. Our hero, on being released from arrest, had sought Mr. Preston, and the latter obligingly agreed to go with him to Tiffany's, and certify to his honesty, that, if the ring should be brought there, it might be retained for him. Paul did not recognize the clerk, but the latter at once remembered him.

"Are you not the boy that brought a diamond ring into our store this morning?" he asked.

"Into Tiffany's?"

"Yes."

"Have you seen anything of it?" asked our hero, eagerly. "I am the one who brought it in."

"A man just brought it into the store," said the clerk.

"Is he there now?"

"He is talking with Mr. Tiffany. I came out for a policeman. He will be arrested at once."

"Good!" exclaimed Paul; "I am in luck. I thought I should never see the ring again. What sort of a man is he?"

From the description, Paul judged that it was Felix Montgomery himself, and, remembering what a trick the adventurer had played upon him at Lovejoy's Hotel, he felt no little satisfaction in the thought that the trapper was himself trapped at last.

"I'll go along with you," he said. "I want to see that man arrested."

"You had better stay outside just at first, until we have secured him."

Meanwhile Mr. Tiffany, after a prolonged examination, said: "The ring is worth two hundred and fifty dollars."

"That will be satisfactory," said Mr. Montgomery, promptly.

"Shall I give you a check for the amount?" asked the jeweler.

"I should prefer the money, as I am a stranger in the city, and not known at the banks."

"I can make the check payable to bearer, and then you will have no difficulty in getting it cashed."

While this conversation was going on, the clerk entered the store with the policeman, but Mr. Montgomery's back was turned, and he was not aware of the fact till the officer tapped him on the shoulder, saying: "You are my prisoner."

"What does this mean? There is some mistake," said the adventurer, wheeling round with a start.

"No mistake at all. You must come with me."

"What have I done? You take me for some one else."

"You have stolen a diamond ring."

"Who says so?" demanded the adventurer, boldly. "It is true I brought one here to sell, but it has belonged to me for years."

"You are mistaken, Mr. Montgomery," said Paul, who had come up unperceived. "You stole that ring from me this morning, after dosing me with chloroform at Lovejoy's Hotel."

"It is a lie," said the adventurer, boldly. "That boy is my son. He is in league with his mother to rob me. She sent him here this morning unknown to me. Finding it out, I took the ring from him, and brought it here myself."

Paul was certainly surprised at being claimed as a son by the man who had swindled him, and answered: "I never saw you before this morning. I have no father living."

"I will guarantee this boy's truth and honesty," said Mr. Preston, speaking for the first time. "I believe you know me, Mr. Tiffany."

"I need no other assurance," said the jeweler, bowing. "Officer, you may remove your prisoner."

"The game is up," said the adventurer, finding no further chance for deception. "I played for high stakes, and I have lost the game. I have one favor to ask. Will some one let my wife know where I am?"

"Give me her address," said Paul, "and I will let her know."

"No. —— Amity Street. Ask her to come to the station-house to see me."

"I will go at once."

"Thank you," said Mr. Montgomery; "as I am not to have the ring, I don't know that I am sorry it has fallen into your hands. One piece of advice I will venture to offer you, my lad," he added, smiling. "Beware of any jewelers hailing from Syracuse. They will cheat you, if you give them a chance."

"I will be on my guard," said Paul. "Can I do anything more for you?"

"Nothing, thank you. I have a fast friend at my side, who will look after me."

The officer smiled grimly at the jest, and the two left the store arm in arm.

"Do you still wish to sell this ring?" asked Mr. Tiffany, addressing Paul.

"Yes, sir."

"I renew my offer of this morning. I will give you two hundred and fifty dollars."

"I shall be glad to accept it."

The sale was quickly effected, and Paul left the store with what seemed to him a fortune in his pocket.

"Be careful not to lose your money," said Mr. Preston.

———

"I should like to place a hundred and fifty dollars in your hands," said Paul, turning to Mr. Preston.

"I will willingly take care of it for you, and allow you interest upon it."

The transfer was made, and, carefully depositing the balance of the money in his pocketbook, our hero took leave of his friend and sought the house in Amity Street.

CHAPTER XXV

PAUL'S FINAL SUCCESS

Mrs. Montgomery impatiently awaited the return of her husband. Meanwhile she commenced packing the single trunk which answered both for her husband and herself. She was getting tired of New York, and anxious to leave for Philadelphia, being fearful lest certain little transactions in which she and her husband had taken part should become known to the police.

She had nearly completed her packing when Paul rang the doorbell.

The summons was answered by the landlady in person.

"Is Mrs. Montgomery at home?" asked Paul.

"No such lady lives here," was the answer.

It occurred to Paul as very possible that Mr. Montgomery might pass under a variety of names. He accordingly said, "Perhaps I have got the name wrong. The lady I mean is tall. I come with a message from her husband, who is a stout man with black hair and whiskers. He gave me this number."

"Perhaps you mean Mr. Grimsby. He and his wife live here."

"Probably that is the name," said Paul.

"I will give Mrs. Grimsby your message," returned the landlady, whose curiosity was excited to learn something further about her boarders.

"Thank you," said Paul; "but it is necessary for me to see the lady myself."

"Well, you can follow me, then," said the landlady, rather ungraciously.

She led the way upstairs, and knocked at the door of Mrs. Grimsby, or as we will still call her, Mrs. Montgomery, since that name is more familiar to the reader, and she was as much entitled to the one as the other.

Mrs. Montgomery opened the door, and regarded our hero suspiciously, for her mode of life had taught her suspicion of strangers.

"Here's a boy that wants to see you," said the landlady.

"I come with a message from your husband," said Paul.

129

Mrs. Montgomery remembered Paul as the boy who was the real owner of the diamond ring, and she eyed him with increased suspicion.

"Did my husband send you? When did you see him."

"Just now, at Tiffany's," answered Paul, significantly.

"What is his message?" asked Mrs. Montgomery, beginning to feel uneasy.

Paul glanced at the landlady, who, in the hope of gratifying her curiosity, maintained her stand by his side.

"The message is private," he said.

"I suppose that means that I am in the way," remarked the landlady, sharply. "I don't want to pry into anybody's secrets. Thank Heaven, I haven't got any secrets of my own."

"Walk in, young man," said Mrs. Montgomery.

Paul entered the room, and she closed the door behind him. Meanwhile the landlady, who had gone part way downstairs, retraced her steps, softly, and put her ear to the keyhole. Her curiosity, naturally strong, had been stimulated by Paul's intimation that there was a secret.

"Now," said Mrs. Montgomery, impatiently, "out with it! Why does my husband send a message by you, instead of coming himself?"

"He can't come himself."

"Why can't he?"

"I am sorry to say that I am the bearer of bad news," said Paul, gravely. "Your husband has been arrested for robbing me of a diamond ring."

"Where is he?" demanded Mrs. Montgomery, not so much excited or overcome as she would have been had this been the first time her husband had fallen into the clutches of the law.

"At the street station-house. He wants you to come and see him."

"Have you got the ring back?"

"Yes."

Mrs. Montgomery was sorry to hear it. She hoped her husband might be able to secrete it, in which case he would pass it over to her to dispose of. Now she was rather awkwardly situated, being without money, or the means of making any.

"I will go," she said.

Paul, who was sitting next to the door, opened it suddenly, with unexpected effort, for the landlady, whose ear was fast to the keyhole, staggered into the room involuntarily.

"So you were listening, ma'am, were you?" demanded Mrs. Montgomery, scornfully.

"Yes, I was," said the landlady, rather red in the face.

"You were in good business."

"It's a better business than stealing diamond rings," retorted the landlady, recovering herself. "I've long suspected there was something wrong about you and your husband, ma'am, and now I know it. I don't want no thieves nor jail birds in my house, and the sooner you pay your bill and leave, the better I'll like it."

"I'll leave as soon as you like, but I can't pay your bill."

"I dare say," retorted the landlady. "You're a nice character to cheat an honest woman out of four weeks' board."

"Well, Paul, what news?" asked Barry.

"I am ready to buy your stand," said Paul.

"Can you pay me all the money down?"

"On the spot."

"Then it is all settled," said Barry, with satisfaction. "I am glad of it, for now I shall be able to go on to Philadelphia tomorrow."

Paul drew a roll of bills from his pocket, and proceeded to count out thirty-five dollars. Barry noticed with surprise that he had a considerable amount left.

"You are getting rich, Paul," he said.

"I am not rich yet," answered Paul, "but I mean to be some time if I can accomplish it by industry and attention to business."

"You'll be sure to succeed," said George Barry. "You're just the right sort. Good-by, old fellow. When you come on to Philadelphia come and see me."

"I may establish a branch stand in Philadelphia before long," said Paul, jocosely.

CHAPTER XXVI

CONCLUSION

When Paul was left in charge of the stand, and realized that it was his own, he felt a degree of satisfaction that can be imagined. He had been a newsboy, a baggage-smasher, and in fact had pretty much gone the round of the street trades, but now he felt that he had advanced one step higher. Some of my readers may not appreciate the difference, but to Paul it was a great one. He was not a merchant prince, to be sure, but he had a fixed place of business, and with his experience he felt confident he could make it pay.

"I am sure I can make from ten to fifteen dollars a week," he said to himself. "I averaged over a dollar a day when I worked for George Barry, and then I only got half-profits. Now I shall have the whole."

This consideration was a very agreeable one. He would be able to maintain his mother and little Jimmy in greater comfort than before, and this he cared more for than for any extra indulgences for himself. In fact, he could relieve his mother entirely from the necessity of working, and yet live better than at present. When Paul thought of this, it gave him a thrill of satisfaction, and made him feel almost like a man.

He set to work soliciting custom, and soon had sold three neckties at twenty-five cents each.

"All that money is mine," he thought, proudly. "I haven't got to hand any of it over to George Barry. That's a comfort."

As this thought occurred to him he recognized an old acquaintance strolling along the sidewalk in his direction. It was no other than Jim Parker, the friend and crony of Mike Donovan, who will be remembered as figuring in not a very creditable way in the earlier chapters of this story. It so happened that he and Paul had not met for some time, and Jim was quite ignorant of Paul's rise in life.

As for Jim himself, no great change had taken place in his appearance or prospects. His suit was rather more ragged and dirty than when we first made his acquaintance, having been worn night and day in the streets, by night stretched out in some dirty alley or out-of-the-way corner, where Jim found cheap lodgings. He strolled along with his hands in his pockets, not much concerned at the deficiencies in his costume.

"Hallo!" said he, stopping opposite Paul's stand. "What are you up to?"

"You can see for yourself," answered Paul. "I am selling neckties."

"How long you've been at it?"

"Just begun."

"Who's your boss?"

"I haven't any."

"You ain't runnin' the stand yourself, be you?" asked Jim, in surprise.

"Yes."

"Where'd you borrow the stamps?"

"Of my mother," said Paul. "Can't I sell you a necktie this morning?"

"Not much," said Jim, laughing at the joke. "I've got my trunks stuffed full of 'em at home, but I don't wear 'em only Sundays. Do you make much money?"

"I expect to do pretty well."

"What made you give up sellin' prize packages?" asked Jim slyly.

"Customers like you," answered Paul.

Jim laughed.

"You didn't catch me that time you lost your basket," he said.

"That was a mean trick," said Paul, indignantly.

"You don't want to hire me to sell for you, do you?"

"That's where you're right. I don't."

"I'd like to go into the business."

"You'd better open a second-hand clothing store," suggested Paul, glancing at his companion's ragged attire.

"Maybe I will," said Jim with a grin, "if you'll buy of me."

"I don't like the style," said Paul. "Who's your tailor?"

"He lives round in Chatham Street. Say, can't you lend a fellow a couple of shillin' to buy some breakfast?"

"Have you done any work to-day?"

"No."

"Then you can't expect to eat if you don't work."

"I didn't have no money to start with."

"Suppose you had a quarter, what would you do?"

"I'd buy a ten-cent plate of meat, and buy some evenin' papers with the rest."

"If you'll do that, I'll give you what you ask for."

"You'll give me two shillin'?" repeated Jim, incredulously, for he remembered how he had wronged Paul.

"Yes," said Paul. "Here's the money;" and he drew a twenty-five-cent piece from his vest pocket, and handed it to Jim.

"You give me that after the mean trick I played you?" said Jim.

"Yes; I am sorry for you and want to help you along."

"You're a brick!" exclaimed Jim, emphatically. "If any feller tries to play a trick on you, you just tell me, and I'll lam him."

"All right, Jim!" said Paul, kindly; "I'll remember it."

"There ain't anybody you want licked, is there?" asked Jim, earnestly.

"Not at present, thank you," said Paul, smiling.

"When you do, I'm on hand," said Jim. "Now I'll go and get some grub."

He shuffled along toward Ann Street, where there was a cheap eating-house, in which ten cents would pay for a plate of meat. He was decidedly hungry, and did justice to the restaurant, whose style of cookery, though not very choice, suited him so well that he could readily have eaten three plates of meat instead of one, but for the prudent thought that compelled him to reserve enough to embark in business afterwards. Jim was certainly a hard ticket; but Paul's unexpected kindness had won him, and produced a more profound impression than a dozen floggings could have done. I may add that Jim proved luck in his business investment, and by the close of the afternoon had enough money to provide himself with supper and lodging, besides a small fund to start with the next day.

Paul sold three more neckties, and then, though it yet lacked an hour of the time when he generally proposed to close, he prepared to go home. He wanted to communicate the good news to his mother and little Jimmy.

Mrs. Hoffman raised her eyes from her sewing as he entered.

"Well, Paul," she said, "have you heard anything of the ring?"

"Yes, mother, it's sold."

"Is it? Well, we must do without it, then," said his mother in a tone of disappointment.

"There won't be any trouble about that, mother, as long as we have got the money for it. I would rather have that than the ring."

"Did you recover it, then?" asked his mother, eagerly.

"Yes, mother—listen and I will tell you all about it."

He sat down and told the story to two very attentive listeners.

"What did you do with the money, Paul?" asked Jimmy.

"Mr. Preston is keeping a hundred and fifty dollars for me. He will allow seven per cent interest. But I must not forget that the money belongs to you, mother, and not to me. Perhaps you would prefer to deposit it in a savings bank."

"I am quite satisfied with your disposal of it, Paul," said Mrs. Hoffman. "I little thought, when I found the ring, that it would be of such service to us."

"It has set me up in business," said Paul, "and I am sure to make money. But I am getting out of stock. I must go round and buy some more neckties to-morrow."

"How much do you pay for your ties, Paul?" asked his mother.

"One shilling; I sell them for two. That gives me a good profit."

"I wonder whether I couldn't make them?" said Mrs. Hoffman. "I find there is no sewing at present to be got, and, besides," she added, "I think I would rather work for you than for a stranger."

"There is no need of your working, mother. I can earn enough to support the family."

"While I have health I would prefer to work, Paul."

"Then I will bring round some of the ties to-morrow. I have two or three kinds. There is nothing very hard about any of them. I think they would be easy to make."

"That will suit me much better than making shirts."

"Suppose I admit you to the firm, mother? I can get a large signboard, and have painted on it:

PAUL HOFFMAN AND MOTHER,
DEALERS IN NECKTIES.

How would that sound?"

"I think I would leave the business part in your hands, Paul."

"I begin to feel like a wholesale merchant already," said Paul. "Who knows but I may be one some day?"

"Many successful men have begun as low down," said his mother; "with energy and industry much may be accomplished."

"Do you think I'll ever be a wholesale painter?" asked Jimmy, whose small ears had drank in the conversation.

"Better try for it, Jimmy," said Paul. "I don't know exactly what a wholesale painter is, unless it's one who paints houses."

"I shouldn't like that," said the little boy.

"Then, Jimmy, you'd better be a retail painter."

"I guess I will," said Jimmy, seriously.

Note: Thus far we have accompanied Paul Hoffman in his career. He is considerably better off than when we met him peddling prize packages in front of the post office. But we have reason to believe that greater success awaits him. He will figure in the next two volumes of this series, more particularly in the second, to be called "Slow and Sure; or, From the Sidewalk to the Shop." Before this appears, however, I propose to describe the adventures of a friend and protegee of Paul's—under the title of PHIL THE FIDDLER.

A woman dealing with a pawnbroker.

~ ~ ~

TEACHERS GUIDE QUESTIONS FOR PAUL THE PEDDLER

1.   When we first meet Paul, he's selling prize packages to people in front of a post office. Is this honest work? Why or why not?

2.   Paul soon finds himself in competition with another prize package salesman. What's the difference between Paul's business and his competition?

3.   Describe Paul's relationship with his family. How does his family figure into his dreams?

4.   Paul's younger brother Jimmy suggests a way for Paul to be more successful with his prize packages. What suggestion does Jimmy make, and how do Paul and his mother react to it? What does this tell you about Paul's family?

5.   Paul takes over George Barry's business while he's recovering from a fever. He makes less money than he did selling packages, but is this a better job? Why or why not?

6.   Mr. Preston takes quite an interest in Paul's story. What comparisons can you draw between Paul and Mr. Preston, and why is he so willing to help Paul?

7.   Paul's mother gives him a ring to sell. Why are they selling the ring? How much could they get from the pawn shop, and how much could they get from the jewelry store? What is the author trying to say about the two people who try to buy the ring?

8.   Who is Felix Montgomery, and why does he do what he does to Paul?

9.   Compare Paul's outcome against the outcomes of Teddy, Felix Montgomery, Mike Donovan and Jerry. What makes Paul successful while the other four fail?

10.   What lesson is the author trying to teach in this story?

TEACHERS GUIDE ANSWERS FOR PAUL THE PEDDLER

1.   Paul had only one package with a ten-cent stamp prize, however, the other prizes were filled with no more than two cents or cheap candy; all in which he would charge a customer five cents just to open each prize.

2.   Teddy had a larger grand prize than Paul. For five cents, a customer could win up to fifty-cents. Teddy also had more than one fifty-cent winner which allowed customers to believe he wasn't conning them into buying a prize but increasing the probability to win.

3.   Paul lives with his mother and his younger brother Jimmy where he supports the household income in lieu of his father's death. Although they cannot contribute as much as he can, Paul's family is very supportive of his efforts to be successful.

4.   Jimmy suggests that Paul play the same trick Teddy was playing, offering a large prize for a decoy to win to draw customers in. Paul and his mother both prefer to make money honestly instead of by using tricks. This tells us the family is honest and hard-working.

5.   It is a better job. Paul can use his sales skills to make more money than his prize packages.

6.   Mr. Preston takes quite an interest in Paul's story. What comparisons can you draw between Paul and Mr. Preston, and why is he so willing to help Paul?

7.   Paul's mother gives him the ring to sell to support the family. The pawn shop offers Paul twenty five dollars, and the jewelry store offers two hundred and fifty dollars. The author is showing that the pawn shop owner is dishonest and was trying to cheat Paul.

8.   Felix Montgomery is a bully. He frames Paul for stealing a watch he stole.

9.   Paul worked hard and honestly while the other four scammed and tried to cheat to get ahead.

10.   Honesty and hard work are the keys to success.

THE LIFE AND THEMES OF
HORATIO ALGER, JR.

By Stefan Kanfer

The Merriam-Webster Dictionary devotes one sentence to him: "Of, relating to, or resembling the fiction of Horatio Alger in which success is achieved through self-reliance and hard work."

True as far as it goes, but that sentence reveals nothing about the man or his accomplishment. Then again, other contemporary reference books are just as terse. Not one acknowledges that Alger in his day (circa 1880-1920) was a publishing phenomenon. During those decades, when a sale of 10,000 volumes was deemed a triumph, readers bought more than 200 million copies of Alger's works, placing him in a league with J.K. Rowling and Stephen King.

Alas, today most of his novels—and there are more than 100—are out of print. But not for long. Thanks to the resuscitation efforts of Sumner Books, a division of Creators Syndicate, Alger's best literary productions are being furnished with fresh covers, new fonts and energetic promotion.

Seldom has there been a more relevant illustration of the maxim that what goes around comes around. At the turn of the 19th century, Alger was the standard-bearer of a phenomenally successful experiment in social reform and personal improvement. That movement inspired disadvantaged kids to move on up, leading juvenile delinquents into productive, significant lives. Men as different as Groucho Marx and Ernest Hemingway were fans.

"Horatio Alger's books conveyed a powerful message to me," wrote Marx, "and to many of my young friends as well—that if you worked hard at your trade, the big chance would eventually come. As a child I didn't regard it as a myth, and as an old man I think of it as the story of my life."

Hemingway's sister Marcelline recalled that during their childhood, "There was one summer when Ernest couldn't get enough of Horatio Alger." Not that Alger's boys' books influenced Papa's prose style. But there must have been something in the writer's stress on grit and self-reliance that affected young Ernest, as it did so many of his contemporaries.

By the end of the Roaring Twenties, though, Horatio Alger had become as passé as the Ford Model T. During the Depression he fared no better; Nathaniel West's satirical 1934 novel, A Cool Million, sent Alger's plots in reverse, as the naïve protagonist loses limb after limb seeking success among rapacious capitalists. Decades later, the film adaptation of Hunter Thompson's 1971 novel, Fear and Loathing in Las Vegas, presented the antihero as "Horatio Alger gone mad on drugs in Las Vegas."

What lay behind Alger's ability to enchant so many Americans—and to enrage so many others? The author's story furnishes a trove of clues:

The sickly child of a Unitarian minister in Marlborough, Massachusetts, Horatio, born in 1832, was always the smallest in his class and far from an academic star. Still, his report cards were good enough for admission to Harvard. There his academic prowess was in inverse proportion to his size (5 feet 2 inches). He won prizes, published verse and fiction in undergraduate magazines, and labeled the entire four years a period of "unmixed happiness."

Decades would pass before he found such contentment again. Upon graduation, Horatio attempted to make his way as a writer. After five unsuccessful years, he returned to Harvard, this time to study at the Divinity School. In 1860 the Reverend Horatio Alger was named minister of the First Parish Unitarian Church of Brewster on Cape Cod. Salary: $800 per year. To supplement his meager income, he turned once again to writing. This time, his stories were well-received, and he allowed himself to dream of a dual career of preacher and writer. That's when catastrophe struck.

It was of his own making, if one historian is to be believed. According to this claim, a 13-year-old told his parents that the new parson had made advances to him. An investigation began. Another lad made a similar complaint. Faced with charges of behaving inappropriately, the accused was allowed to resign—with the proviso that he leave town at once.

Sometime later, Horatio wrote a poem about one Friar Anselmo, who had committed an unspecified crime. Melancholy and remorseful, he comes across a wounded traveler and gives him aid. Whereupon an angel materializes and offers salvation:

Thy guilty stains shall be washed white again
By noble service done thy fellow man.

The fugitive repaired to New York City in the spring of 1866, resolved to live out the Christian ideal, expiating his sin by saving others. The Manhattan he entered was the epicenter of the Gilded Age, a magnet for millions of ambitious climbers, drawn by the post-Civil War boom. Out of sight of the glittering prosperity, the mansions and carriages, however, was another New York, a squalid night town that travelers compared to Calcutta, India.

In The Good Old Days, They Were Terrible, historian Otto Bettmann reports that there was scarcely a slum that pedestrians could negotiate "without climbing over a heap of trash or, in rain, wading through a bed of slime." Many streets were so dangerous that policemen hesitated to walk them alone. A Gramercy Park resident noted in his diary, "Most of my friends are investing in revolvers and carry them about at night"—and the Park was one of the city's better neighborhoods.

The New York City street urchin entered the national consciousness in those years. More than 60,000 neglected or abandoned kids ran unsupervised in the street, partly because of the fallout from the tidal waves of immigration from Europe and partly because of families broken by the Civil War.

What was to be done about these juveniles likely to die on the streets or to end up behind bars? The Reverend Charles Loring Brace founded the Children's Aid Society, designed to take homeless or abused kids away from their corrosive environments. At the same time, John Hughes, New York's first Roman Catholic archbishop, set up parochial schools and a residential institution called the Catholic Protectory, which brought up abandoned or orphaned children to be useful members of society.

Horatio Alger joined these efforts at reclamation. He, too, asked himself what could be done about homeless children. Seeking answers, he wandered through the city's worst neighborhoods. He interviewed "street arabs" who spoke of broken homes, violent confrontations with parents, doomed futures. He observed how their cocky attitudes masked a profound despair. He advised them to get real jobs instead of hanging about, squandering whatever came their way from shining shoes or picking pockets. A handful nodded in agreement, expressing the desire to change their lives; most were content to take life as they found it.

Why, he pondered, did individuals subjected to the same conditions turn out so differently? One boy might become a thief, a sociopath, even a killer. His neighbor, perhaps his brother, might aim to be an upright citizen. What was the difference between them?

What saved certain boys, he came to believe, was a quality that gave them the strength to resist sloth and temptation. In a word, character. But was this inborn? In that case determinism won the day, and change was out of the question. Or, given the right opportunity and attitude, could a dispossessed youth win his share of the American dream? The latter, Alger believed—but only if the boy stopped regarding himself as a victim.

As Alger meditated upon the worst crime of the slums—the stealing of childhood from children—an idea came to him. He would be Brother Anselmo redivivus. He had sinned against youths; now he would rescue them—and in the process save himself. As the novelist put it, by depicting the situation of city waifs, he would "excite a deeper and more widespread sympathy in the public mind, as well as exert a salutary influence upon the class of whom he is writing, by setting before them inspiring examples of what energy, ambition, and an honest purpose may achieve."

Ragged Dick became the template of the fiction to follow. Subtitled Street Life in New York with the Boot Blacks, it charted the rise of a 14-year-old boy from poverty to prosperity. Dick Hunter is an adolescent with all odds against him. He has no family, he smokes, drinks alcohol when he can afford it—not very often on the small change he gets from shining gentlemen's shoes—and sleeps on gratings in the winter.

Yet something separates him from his fellow waifs. He refuses to pick pockets like the others, won't mock his elders, and yearns to "grow up 'spectable.'" His bearing and his innate decency attract the attention of upright New Yorkers. One introduces him to his church; another presents Dick with a few dollars.

The earnest youth resolves to become literate to save his money and live a clean life. One day on a walk near South Ferry he sees a toddler fall in the water. Without hesitation, Dick jumps in and saves the drowning child. In gratitude, the father, an affluent businessman, offers the rescuer a job in his office. Gainfully employed, the onetime vagabond Dick Hunter becomes Richard Hunter Esq., and shuts the door forever on the "old vagabond life which he hoped never to resume."

Naïve? Simplistic? To the jaded, the cynical and the ignorant, yes. But not to thousands of children trapped in the real world of poverty and early death. They got the message of Ragged Dick and demanded more Horatio Alger novels with more moral lessons for them to absorb. Those books changed—and in many cases saved—lives a century before Dr. Martin Luther King Jr. stated his belief that what mattered was not the color of one's skin but the content of one's character.

Today, if you listen closely you can hear, amid the jeers, the escalating sound of the last laugh. In 1947, the Horatio Alger Association was founded. It attracts more prominent men and women now than it did then. The group is dedicated to recognizing American leaders who rose, like Alger's young heroes, from humble origins "through honesty, hard work, self-reliance and perseverance." With grants to U.S. high-school students who have "faced and overcome great obstacles in their young lives," the association encourages them to emulate such enterprising and disparate members as Oprah Winfrey and Ray Kroc, Tom Brokaw and Maya Angelou, Stan Musial and Colin Powell.

They can all testify to the truths that lie between the covers of this volume. Turn the first few pages, and you'll understand why so many followed Horatio Alger's breathless, cliff-hanging chapters leading the way from skid row to success. And why so many more are about to read that map in a world where everything has changed—except the basic truths of life.

Stefan Kanfer is an award-winning writer for City Journal and the author of numerous best-selling books.

ABOUT HORATIO ALGER, JR.

Horatio Alger was born in 1832 in Chelsea, Massachusetts. He spent his early years in the small town and under the guidance of the church and his father, the town pastor, before the family moved just west of Boston to the town of Marlborough.

As a shy young boy, Alger poured himself into books and soon became a distinguished student. He studied at Harvard and Harvard Divinity School before becoming a minister. He practiced ministry for a few years near Boston and on Cape Cod, but he was distracted by his true passion: writing.

He loved to write, and by 1865 Alger had written a handful of stories, including Frank's Campaign and Paul Prescott's Charge. The latter was the first in a series of stories that would eventually lead to his great success. In 1866, Alger moved to New York to write poetry, newspaper stories and magazine articles. However, he was shocked to find so many homeless and forgotten children among the streets, an unfortunate consequence of the Civil War. He made it his duty to aid the condition of these lost children, both through his stories and by his continuous acts of benevolence.

Horatio Alger became a household name shortly after the Civil War when he began publishing stories in the form of serializations. These serializations were featured in magazines such as Student and Schoolmate and were later compiled as books. Alger's books became enormously popular, especially among teenage boys across the country, and they soon reached millions and millions of readers. Alger continued to produce several stories a year, and, in later years, wrote novels in and of themselves instead of novels from magazine serials.

The years immediately following the Civil War were the same years when the United States emerged as one nation on the road to becoming a worldwide empire. The years between 1865 and 1900 were the years of the empire builders, with the rags-to-riches stories of John D. Rockefeller, Andrew Carnegie, Cornelius Vanderbilt and Thomas Edison. They were the years that laid the foundation for Henry Ford and other business titans and for the spectacular growth of the American economy throughout the 20th century and through today. During these years, Alger published well over 100 stories, poems and novels that spoke to the timeless themes and successes of this era.

The theme of Alger's books is consistent: If you work hard, go the extra mile, are faithful and honest, show kindness and generosity, and maintain a cheerful, positive and optimistic attitude, you will succeed in creating financial security and happiness. On the other hand, if you lie, cheat, steal, are lazy or envious, and try to take advantage of other people, you will be doomed to failure and misery. Despite his background as a preacher, Alger does not make these points in a self-righteous or pontificating way. What he does instead -- just like the parables that Jesus told -- is to create stories that illustrate the virtues that lead to success. And the stories that Alger creates are no ordinary stories. Each one is filled with lively plots and twists and turns, ones that are always unexpected and keep the reader wanting to know what's going to happen next.

As Alger grew older, he continuously strived to write the Great American Novel, little realizing that the rags-to-riches stories he created were more influential than any other novelists'. He travelled out west in early 1877 searching for new material and returned near the end of the year, producing similar stories with a new western backdrop. By 1897, Alger was suffering from asthma, bronchitis and slight short-term memory loss. He moved in with his sister in South Natick, Massachusetts where he spent the last two years of his life.

Most people have never heard of Horatio Alger while some are vaguely familiar with the term "rags-to-riches." In the Alger family, it was the norm to burn correspondence and manuscripts, and this, coupled with Alger's shyness, has greatly kept him from history's limelight. Though too often forgotten today, Alger's works and the themes within them still affect the American psyche. Many assert that there is a lagging spirit in present American culture, that these inspiring stories are irrelevant. Young people are bombarded with external stimuli that make it difficult for them to get to know themselves. Wide-eyed innocence and childlike enthusiasm, once revered as admirable qualities, are sources of mockery and disdain, which makes cynicism and pessimism inevitable. Video games, television shows, movies and music are all aimed at titillating and at seeing who can be the most gritty, violent or shocking. More than a few commentators have used the word "degrading" to describe the assault that children encounter today.

This is unfortunate. Young people need heroes and role models today just as much as they did in the 1870s and '80s, when Alger was creating them at a feverish pace from his New York City apartment, writing as many as four books at a time. Publisher A.K. Loring asserted that Alger's books "captured the spirits of reborn America" for "above all you can hear the cry of triumph of the oppressed over the oppressor ... What Alger has done is to portray the soul – the ambitious soul – of the country." Years later, biographer Edwin P. Hoyt concludes that Alger is "a writer whose influence on the American scene has been so profound that it is hard to measure." Indeed, Alger's works made an overwhelming impression on American culture and society that are still alive with us today. It is for this reason that these classics must be brought to a new generation of readers.

OUR COMMITMENT TO
HORATIO ALGER

By Rick Newcombe

Sumner Books is totally committed to reviving interest in Horatio Alger, one of the best-selling authors of all time yet someone who has been all but forgotten today. I'd like to tell you how this project came about.

Probably the best starting point is to tell you a little about myself. I grew up in suburban Chicago, and my parents were religious and fundamentally optimistic in their outlook on life. They encouraged all eight of their children to be positive in our thinking and hope and pray for the best in all situations. In my adolescence, I discovered many of the self-help authors from the 20th century, including Dale Carnegie, Napoleon Hill and Norman Vincent Peale. I remember reading a small magazine in the 1970s, when I was in my 20s, called Success Unlimited and being inspired each month to work hard and stay positive. The publisher of this magazine was W. Clement Stone, who started his career selling insurance policies door to door and who went on to build Combined Insurance, which became part of Aon, one of the largest insurance companies in the world.

By the time Mr. Stone died in 2002, he was a very successful businessman, an extremely generous philanthropist and totally committed to spreading the gospel of positive thinking. I remember reading one of his books, The Success System That Never Fails, which was both an autobiography and a blueprint for achieving success. Stone told the story of spending a summer on a farm in Michigan when he was 12, getting fresh air, helping on the farm and enjoying picnics, carnivals and camping out.

W. Clement Stone

"But I'll never forget the first day I went upstairs to the attic," he wrote, "for there I met Horatio Alger. At least 50 of his books, dusty and weather-worn, were piled in the corner. I took one down to the hammock in the front yard and started to read."

Stone said he was so enthralled he couldn't stop. "I read through all of them that summer," he wrote.

He said the principle in each book was that "the hero became a success because he was a man of character -- the villain a failure because he deceived and embezzled. How many Alger books were sold? No one knows. Estimates range from 100 million to 300 million. We do know that his books inspired thousands of American boys from poor families to strive to do the right thing because it was right and to acquire wealth."

That was the first time I had heard of Horatio Alger, but it never occurred to me to try to find his books. Over the years, I founded Creators Syndicate, which became one of the most successful newspaper syndication companies in the world. I attribute much of our success to our positive thinking and upbeat attitude. We became a multimillion-dollar international corporation by syndicating a wide variety of journalists, celebrities and award-winning cartoonists.

As we were expanding into new businesses, e-books and audiobooks were a natural starting point because we work with so many talented writers and artists. But we also wanted to try new things. With that in mind, I remembered Mr. Stone's enthusiastic recommendation of Horatio Alger's books, and I decided to read some. Many were available as e-books, and I thoroughly enjoyed them.

I had a good feeling whenever I was transported back to New York City as it was in 1870, when trains were called "cars" and there were no automobiles. There was a constant risk of crossing the streets without streetlights or walk signs. A number of years later, the Brooklyn Dodgers, now the Los Angeles Dodgers, got their name from the treacherous dodging of horses, wagons and streetcars that was required to cross the street in the city. In those days, plumbing with hot and cold running water was not taken for granted, much less radios, televisions, computers or smartphones. Are you kidding? A smartphone in the 1860s? There wasn't even a telephone.

But what great stories Alger wrote -- one after another. I couldn't get enough of them! And it was impossible not to feel grateful for all the modern conveniences of the 21st century when immersing myself in the world of America as it was in the 1860s and '70s.

As I read book after book, I felt like a teenager all over again, excited about the future and the promise of a brighter tomorrow. It was then that I decided to go full bore into spreading the word of Horatio Alger.

One of the problems with the e-books was the lack of organization; another was the maddening number of typos, over and over and over, or the lack of illustrations or the lack of a table of contents. In fact, what was intended to be a good deed to spread Mr. Alger's message really turned out to be something of a disservice.

So I made it my mission to have professional editors edit the texts so there were no typographical or spelling errors. We found appropriate illustrations. We included detailed tables of contents for each book, and we decided to publish them in groups, when appropriate, which has never been done before. We are including commentaries and teachers guides with each e-book.

We also decided to make audiobooks of as many of these "Stories of Success" as possible. We hired a terrific actor, Ben Gillman, and his initial experience shows you how far we have to go to spread the word. Ben went to the Hollywood public library to find some Horatio Alger books, but there was none. "You'd have to go to the downtown public library, in the historical section, to find those," the librarian told him.

Remember, this is one of the best-selling American authors of all time, yet it is as if he never existed.

Part of the problem is that some of the caricatures of Horatio Alger over the years have been absolutely brutal. Even to this day, the Encyclopedia Britannica, from which we expect objective reporting, calls Alger's dialogue and plots "outrageously bad." Come again? The encyclopedia is supposed to provide broad knowledge on specific subjects, not offer the biased literary criticism of a handful of editors. Talk about being unfair -- and just plain wrong!

How do you answer a cheap shot like that? Really, it is nothing more than an incredibly snooty opinion; in fact, it is an "outrageously bad" opinion. Remember, the Horatio Alger books were intended to be not great literature but rather inspirational stories to motivate young boys to achieve a better life. If the dialogue and plots were not lively and believable, the books would not have sold in the millions. The fact that Horatio Alger helped form the American character shows that an incredible number of boys ate up his books as thrilling and believable.

The brilliant writer Stefan Kanfer wrote an extensive review of Horatio Alger's works in 2000 for City Journal magazine, a publication of the prestigious Manhattan Institute. He started off believing the critics, but when he actually read some of Horatio Alger's books, he drew a totally different conclusion. "I began reading the novels aloud to my children," he wrote. "We found them well-plotted, entertaining, and instructive, not at all the righteous antiquities that I had been led to believe. Almost every chapter ends with a cliff-hanger, and all of us could hardly wait for the next night to find out what happened. The conclusions never failed to produce an emotional satisfaction and a feeling that what the author was selling -- independence, forbearance, square dealing -- was well worth buying."

We can only speculate about why the critics have been so harsh on Horatio Alger, but no doubt some it stems from their being turned off by precisely the character traits that Mr. Kanfer identifies. Like it or not, there is a mindset that scoffs at individual achievement through hard work, a positive attitude and generosity -- living every day with an "attitude of gratitude," which is the essence of Horatio Alger's message.

W. Clement Stone was routinely mocked for starting the day by saying, "I feel healthy! I feel happy! I feel terrific!" He encouraged his employees to do the same. In fact, he encouraged everyone to demonstrate outward enthusiasm and PMA, which stood for a positive mental attitude. His critics thought he was ridiculous, but Mr. Stone got the last laugh, living to age 100, which he had set as his goal, and accumulating hundreds of millions of dollars.

Roswell Crawford is an important character in Ragged Dick and Fame and Fortune because he oozes the world-owes-me-a-living attitude that is so common today. "Roswell was troubled with a large share of pride," Alger writes, "though it might have troubled himself to explain what he had to be proud of."

Roswell never understands the importance of integrity and its relationship to earning one's living. In fact, he once says that he would be happy to be paid $10 a week for nothing. "Well, if I get it, I don't care if I don't earn it," he says. In fact, Roswell is ashamed to be seen in the streets carrying a large bundle as part of a delivery for his job. Before being fired, his boss tells him, "You appear to think yourself of too great consequence to discharge properly the duties of your position."

Contrast that with Richard Hunter's attitude toward his entry-level job when he first starts working at the firm. "I'm ready to do anything that is required of me. I want to make myself useful," he says.

I have the impression that was the same attitude that Horatio Alger had as he approached his goal of becoming a successful writer who could change the world -- or at least the world of the thousands of homeless street urchins in the big city. It is difficult to imagine how bad their plight was. For instance, in 1874, which was seven years after Ragged Dick was first published, there was a little girl named Mary Ellen Wilson, who was beaten unmercifully by her stepmother. She was sent out into the streets ill-clothed in winter. There were other abuses, and they were horrible.

So a social worker named Etta Angel Wheeler wanted to intervene, to help get the child out of that environment. But there were no laws to protect children in such situations. Etta was desperate -- and clever. She enlisted the help of the American Society for the Prevention of Cruelty to Animals because animals were protected by law. Her attorneys argued that Mary Ellen, "as a member of the animal kingdom, deserved the same protection as abused animals." This led to new legislation and various child protective services.

Horatio Alger was at the forefront of this movement. He wanted to help the poor kids in the inner city, and he wound up not only helping them but inspiring millions of other young readers across the country. Many of them transformed their lives as a direct result of the inspiration of the "Stories of Success" that Horatio Alger managed to tell in one exciting setting after another.

It is not surprising that Ernest Hemingway's sister said that her brother could not get enough of Horatio Alger or that Walter Brennan, a famous actor for much of the 20th century, devoured his books. As the legendary Groucho Marx said: "Horatio Alger's books conveyed a powerful message to me and to many of my young friends -- that if you worked hard at your trade, the big chance would eventually come. As a child, I didn't regard it as a myth, and as an old man, I think of it as the story of my life."

Groucho was speaking for millions of Americans in the past and, we hope, millions more in the future.

Rick Newcombe is the founder and CEO of Creators Syndicate, Creators Publishing and Sumner Books.

PREVIEW OF ANOTHER ADVENTURE IN THE HORATIO ALGER "STORIES OF SUCCESS" SERIES

PHIL THE FIDDLER

"Viva Garibaldi!" sang a young Italian boy in an uptown street, accompanying himself on a violin which, from its battered appearance, seemed to have met with hard usage.

As the young singer is to be the hero of my story, I will pause to describe him. He was twelve years old, but small of his age. His complexion was a brilliant olive, with the dark eyes peculiar to his race, and his hair black. In spite of the dirt, his face was strikingly handsome, especially when lighted up by a smile, as was often the case, for in spite of the hardships of his lot, and these were neither few nor light, Filippo was naturally merry and light-hearted.

He wore a velveteen jacket, and pantaloons which atoned, by their extra length, for the holes resulting from hard usage and antiquity. His shoes, which appeared to be wholly unacquainted with blacking, were, like his pantaloons, two or three sizes too large for him, making it necessary for him to shuffle along ungracefully.

It was now ten o'clock in the morning. Two hours had elapsed since Filippo, or Phil, as I shall call him, for the benefit of my readers unfamiliar with Italian names, had left the miserable home in Crosby Street, where he and forty other boys lived in charge of a middle-aged Italian, known as the padrone. Of this person, and the relations between him and the boys, I shall hereafter speak. At present I propose to accompany Phil.

Though he had wandered about, singing and playing, for two hours, Phil had not yet received a penny. This made him somewhat uneasy, for he knew that at night he must carry home a satisfactory sum to the padrone, or he would be brutally beaten; and poor Phil knew from sad experience that this hard taskmaster had no mercy in such cases.

The block in which he stood was adjacent to Fifth Avenue, and was lined on either side with brown-stone houses. It was quiet, and but few passed through it during the busy hours of the day. But Phil's hope was that some money might be thrown him from a window of some of the fine houses before which he played, but he seemed likely to be disappointed, for he played ten minutes without apparently attracting any attention. He was about to change his position, when the basement door of one of the houses opened, and a servant came out, bareheaded, and approached him. Phil regarded her with distrust, for he was often ordered away as a nuisance. He stopped playing, and, hugging his violin closely, regarded her watchfully.

"You're to come in," said the girl abruptly.

"Che cosa volete?"(1) said Phil, suspiciously.

(1) "What do you want?"

"I don't understand your Italian rubbish," said the girl. "You're to come into the house."

In general, boys of Phil's class are slow in learning English. After months, and even years sometimes, their knowledge is limited to a few words or phrases. On the other hand, they pick up French readily, and as many of them, en route for America, spend some weeks, or months, in the French metropolis, it is common to find them able to speak the language somewhat. Phil, however, was an exception, and could manage to speak English a little, though not as well as he could understand it.

"What for I go?" he asked, a little distrustfully.

"My young master wants to hear you play on your fiddle," said the servant. "He's sick, and can't come out."

"All right!" said Phil, using one of the first English phrases he had caught. "I will go."

"Come along, then."

Phil followed his guide into the basement, thence up two flight of stairs, and along a handsome hall into a chamber. The little fiddler, who had never before been invited into a fine house, looked with admiration at the handsome furniture, and especially at the pictures upon the wall, for, like most of his nation, he had a love for whatever was beautiful, whether in nature or art.

The chamber had two occupants. One, a boy of twelve years, was lying in a bed, propped up by pillows. His thin, pale face spoke of long sickness, and contrasted vividly with the brilliant brown face of the little Italian boy, who seemed the perfect picture of health. Sitting beside the bed was a lady of middle age and pleasant expression. It was easy to see by the resemblance that she was the mother of the sick boy.

Phil looked from one to the other, uncertain what was required of him.

"Can you speak English?" asked Mrs. Leigh.

"Si, signora, a little," answered our hero.

"My son is sick, and would like to hear you play a little."

"And sing, too," added the sick boy, from the bed.

Phil struck up the song he had been singing in the street, a song well known to all who have stopped to listen to the boys of his class, with the refrain, "Viva Garibaldi." His voice was clear and melodious, and in spite of the poor quality of his instrument, he sang with so much feeling that the effect was agreeable.

The sick boy listened with evident pleasure, for he, too, had a taste for music.

"I wish I could understand Italian," he said, "I think it must be a good song."

"Perhaps he can sing some English song," suggested Mrs. Leigh.

"Can you sing in English?" she asked.

Phil hesitated a moment, and then broke into the common street ditty, "Shoe fly, don't bouder me," giving a quaint sound to the words by his Italian accent.

"Do you know any more?" asked Henry Leigh, when our hero had finished.

"Not English," said Phil, shaking his head.

"You ought to learn more."

"I can play more," said Phil, "but I know not the words."

"Then play some tunes."

Thereupon the little Italian struck up "Yankee Doodle," which he played with spirit and evident enjoyment.

"Do you know the name of that?" asked Henry.

Phil shook his head.

"It is 'Yankee Doodle.'"

Phil tried to pronounce it, but the words in his mouth had a droll sound, and made them laugh.

"How old are you?" asked Henry.

"Twelve years."

"Then you are quite as old as I am."

"I wish you were as well and strong as he seems to be," said Mrs. Leigh, sighing, as she looked at Henry's pale face.

156

That was little likely to be. Always a delicate child, Henry had a year previous contracted a cold, which had attacked his lungs, and had gradually increased until there seemed little doubt that in the long struggle with disease nature must succumb, and early death ensue.

"How long have you been in this country?"

"Un anno."

"How long is that?"

"A year," said Henry. "I know that, because 'annus' means a year in Latin."

"Si, signor, a year," said Phil.

"And where do you come from?"

"Da Napoli."

"That means from Naples, I suppose."

"Si, signor."

Most of the little Italian musicians to be found in our streets are brought from Calabria, the southern portion of Italy, where they are purchased from their parents, for a fixed sum, or rate of annual payment. But it is usual for them when questioned, to say that they come from Naples, that being the principal city in that portion of Italy, or indeed in the entire kingdom.

"Who do you live with," continued Henry.

"With the padrone."

"And who is the padrone?"

"He take care of me—he bring me from Italy."

"Is he kind to you?"

Phil shrugged his shoulders.

"He beat me sometimes," he answered.

"Beats you? What for?"

"If I bring little money."

"Does he beat you hard?"

"Si, signor, with a stick."

"He must be a bad man," said Henry, indignantly.

"How much money must you carry home?"

"Two dollars."

"But it isn't your fault, if people will not give you money."

"Non importa. He beat me."

"He ought to be beaten himself."

Phil shrugged his shoulders. Like most boys of his class, to him the padrone seemed all-powerful. The idea that his oppressive taskmaster should be punished for his cruelty had never dawned upon him. Knowing nothing of any law that would protect him, he submitted to it as a necessity, from which there was no escape except by running away. He had not come to that yet, but some of his companions had done so, and he might some day.

After this conversation he played another tune. Mrs. Leigh drew out her purse, and gave him fifty cents. Phil took his fiddle under his arm, and, following the servant, who now reappeared, emerged into the street, and moved onward.

BE SURE TO LISTEN TO THE AUDIOBOOK "STORIES OF SUCCESS" SERIES BY HORATIO ALGER, AVAILABLE ON AUDIBLE.COM AND ITUNES. GO TO WWW.SUMNERBOOKS.COM.

www.ingramcontent.com/pod-product-compliance
Lightning Source LLC
Chambersburg PA
CBHW060927040426
42445CB00011B/837